Praise for the Dating Goddess

The *Adventures in Delicious Dating After 40* series of books is based on the blog Adventures in Delicious Dating After 40 at www.DatingGoddess.com. Here are comments from readers.

- "Adventures in Delicious Dating After 40 is a wonderful composite of both the mechanics of post-40 online dating and what the practice of honoring one's self actually looks like. How marvelous your writing is to read. I spent about 2 hours reading and was riveted the whole time." —Maggie Hanna

- "At last, a dating writer who addresses requirements. You are SO right on! I'm thrilled to have found you!" —Rachel Sarah, author, *Single Mom Seeking*

- "Powerfully heartfelt and honest writing. You are inspiring." —Kare Anderson, Emmy Award winning writer

"I just love your writing. It is very fresh and gives the reader something to think about." —Kelly Lantz, President & Manager, 55-Alive.com

"Dating Goddess, you are like a, a, a, well, a goddess to me. You've helped guide me successfully through my re-entry into the dating world after 14 years. I'm an eager student and fast study, and do get myself into situations that others don't know how to deal with — such as 3 dates in one day -— so thankfully you are there! You're the greatest, thanks for all you do for us!" —Jae G.

"I find your point of view much more interesting than other dating writers. Thanks for always reminding me to enjoy dating life no matter what it throws at you." —Sandy

"I love Adventures in Delicious Dating After 40. I really do like your honest and authentic voice — it's refreshing." —Wendy S.

"Adventures in Delicious Dating After 40 is really fun to read. Thanks for sharing your thoughts and letting us divorced single women know that we are not alone. There's a lot here that I identify with, although I'm not as brave as you are about dating lots of guys. So far. Love your blog — the first blog I've ever read consistently." —Elizabeth

"Thanks for a wonderful blog. You're doing a great job of saying what's in my mind. There's rarely a day I miss when it comes to checking in on your wisdom." —Paulette Ensign

Winning
at the Online
Dating
Game

Stack the Deck
in Your Favor

by **Dating Goddess**

Winning at the Online Dating Game: Stack the Deck in Your Favor

Second Edition

Cover design by Dave Innis, www.innisanimation.com

Book design by JustYourType.biz

Printed in the United States of America.

ISBN

Print: 978-1-930039-37-7

eBook: 978-1-930039-17-9

How to order:

The *Adventures in Delicious Daing After 40* books may be ordered directly from www.DatingGoddess.com.

Quantity discounts are also available. Visit us online for updates and additional articles.

*The Adventures in Delicious
Dating After 40 books are
dedicated to my ex-husband
since he unexpectedly re-
leased me to explore the unte-
thered life of a single woman.
I then had the freedom for the
experiences, lessons and insights shared in these pages.*

Books by Dating Goddess

- *Date or Wait: Are You Ready for Mr. Great?*

- *Assessing Your Assets: Why You're A Great Catch*

- *In Search of King Charming: Who Do I Want to Share My Throne?*

- *Embracing Midlife Men: Insights Into Curious Behaviors*

- *Dipping Your Toe in the Dating Pool: Dive In Without Belly Flopping*

- *Winning at the Online Dating Game: Stack the Deck in Your Favor*

- *Check Him Out Before Going Out: Avoiding Dud Dates*

- *First-Rate First Dates: Increasing the Chances of a Second Date*

- *Real Deal or Faux Beau: Should You Keep Seeing Him?*

- *Multidating Responsibly: Play the Field Without Being A Player*

- *Moving On Gracefully: Break Up Without Heartache*

- *From Fear to Frolic: Get Naked Without Getting Embarrassed*

- *Ironing Out Dating Wrinkles: Work Through Challenges Without Getting Steamed*

Contents

DatingGoddess.com

x

Introduction

This book is designed for anyone who is interested in stories, advice, and lessons from the midlife dating front. If you are over 40 and haven't dated in a while — or even if you have — you'll learn ways to approach dating with zeal, optimism, and hope. Even if you've had more than your share of negative experiences, I'll share how to glean lessons from those adventures, rather than just declaring that "all men are jerks" or "men are just looking for sex."

While most of the perspective is from a woman to women, men's comments, experiences, and lessons have been integrated as appropriate.

This book began as daily entries into my blog, Adventures in Delicious Dating After 40, which has been featured in the *Wall Street Journal* as well as on radio and TV. I wrote about my epiphanies from my and my friends' dating life. The best postings were culled to make this and subsequent books.

This book focuses on the the ins and outs of online dating. How to play the game, which has it's own rules and language. If you don't understand how online dating works, you'll waste a lot of time connecting with men who are not a possible fit for you.

xi

This book consists of three types of perspectives:

Lessons: These are specific experiences I thought would be useful to you. A few lines from my experience illustrate the points.

Insights: These usually start with an experience I've encountered, then the insights that experience spawned. It is usually comprised of around half story and half insight.

Stories: These are examples of situations I've experienced — or was currently experiencing when I wrote that piece — that I thought would be entertaining. Or I thought the story would help you see what kind of things happen in the midlife dating world so you'd know what has happened to others.

Because these writings were real time, as they occured, they are often set in the present tense. But they are not chronological. So a reference to "my current beau" may now be many sweethearts ago. I hope this isn't confusing.

I'd love ot hear your stories and questions. Please email them to me at Goddess@DatingGoddess.com. They may make it into the blog or my next book!

Who is the Dating Goddess?

I am a middle-aged, white, professional woman. My husband of nearly 20 years left me in April 2003 when I was 47, 11 days shy of 48. After giving my heart time to heal from the surprise divorce sprung by the man I thought was my soulmate, I started dating 18 months later. Generally, I have had a great time meeting interesting men, some of whom became romantic beaus, some became treasured friends, and some I never heard from again.

I am not a well-preserved, gorgeous, marathon-running middle-aged women

In the beginning, I had dates with single male colleagues, but I quickly found Internet dating was the way to explore the most "inventory" and qualify men who I thought might be a good match.

I am not one of those well-preserved, gorgeous,

marathon-running middle-aged women. I have been told I am attractive, but I am overweight and not a gym rat. So while I am active, I do not match the description 90% of men's profiles say they want: slender, athletic, toned, fit. I have some wrinkles — what one sweet suitor mistakenly called dimples. I have what Bridget Jones called "wobbly bits," as most non-surgically enhanced middle-aged women do. My genes — and a lifetime addiction to chocolate — have made their mark. Yet I've met and dated some wonderful men, so even if you're not a lingerie model, you can find guys who will think you're attractive, perhaps even hot!

In my professional life, I am a bestselling author of workplace effectiveness books, professional speaker and management consultant. I've appeared on Oprah, 60 Minutes, and National Public Radio and in the *Wall Street Journal* and *USA Today*.

This book is intended to not only be useful to others and cathartic for me, but is also the genesis of a new topic for fun, thought-provoking speeches. I'm calling myself a dating philosopher and giving date-a-vational speeches! Let me know if you know a group who would like an entertaining after-lunch speech on how lessons learned from dating have implications in business and personal relationships and well as life philosophies.

How did I come by the Dating Goddess moniker? After a few months of dating dozens of men — one week yielded 7 dates with 6 guys in 5 days — my friends dubbed me this name. I liked it, so it stuck.

I'm purposefully not sharing my picture as I don't want you to think either, "How did she get any dates at all?" or the opposite, "Of course she found it easy to get 112 men to ask her out." I am not hideous (usually) nor am I stunning (without professional hair, makeup and Photoshop!). Some men find me attractive, some don't.

I continue to search for my "one," but I have learned a lot along the way, and my single and not-single friends have loudly encouraged me to share my experiences and lessons in the hopes of helping others navigate the adventure of dating with more success. And to have a delicious time doing it!

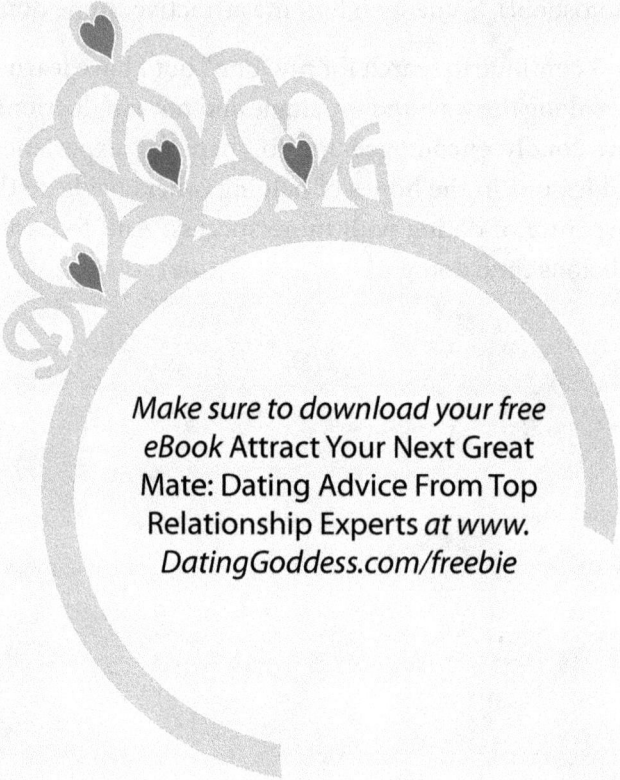

Make sure to download your free eBook Attract Your Next Great Mate: Dating Advice From Top Relationship Experts at www. DatingGoddess.com/freebie

Shopping for men

Dating life can be brutal. You make an effort to look nice (I call it getting "dated up") to meet someone new, then he either doesn't contact you afterwards, tells you he's not attracted to you or there's none of that elusive "chemistry." You have to have perseverance and hope that someone for you is right around the corner — or in the next email.

I've found dating to be a lot like clothes shopping. First, you have to shop where you know there is a large pool of prospects, which is why people shop at malls. When I conduct an online search, I call it "shopping for men." On the best dating sites, you can search by important criteria (e.g., age, height, location, income, education, smoking/non-smoking, even activity level). Just like clothes shopping, you know the size, colors and style you want.

And just like clothes shopping, you have to look at LOTS of possibilities, even when you've narrowed it down to a certain brand and size. It is easy to get frustrated.

After a day of shopping with no buys, do you say "There are no good clothes out there?" Or "All the good clothes are taken!" Or "All the clothes I tried on are losers. I'm giving up. I'm never shopping again!" No. How silly.

Would you ever consider stopping shopping? No. You keep shopping because you have hope that you'll find something you'll love — that will be comfortable and fit and you'll feel great in. Same with guys.

However, it can get wearisome going on a bunch of dates with guys who on paper seem a good match, but in person there's no spark. You can doubt your attractiveness, or think you are too picky. If you find no one you can entertain the possibility of going out with again, then perhaps it is time to reassess your criteria.

For example, I thought I must have a college graduate. Then I dated a delightful gentleman who didn't complete college as he was recruited to be a CEO while in college. He is very bright, but was tapped before completing his degree. I then found other fun men who were successful despite not having a degree.

Did I "settle" for less by lowering my criteria to allow for those who didn't complete college? I don't think so. If you're having a hard time in your shopping activities, consider if some of your criteria could be altered.

It's raining men!

"Ten men waiting for me at the door? Send one of them home. I'm tired." —Mae West

One of the beauties of online dating is it seems there is a never-ending supply of potential suitors. At least that's my experience. And I have pretty stringent criteria for my matches. Yes, I get 10 times more guys winking and emailing who don't come close to matching my criteria. But it seems that weekly I get a few who meet enough criteria to respond to their inquiry.

It is fun to meet new guys, although it can be time consuming, and if you let it, frustrating. Once I had 7 dates with 6 guys in 5 days. It is exhilarating to feel desirable, yet as I've become more experienced, I've become more discerning. Now I see two to four new guys a month, rather than a week.

The downside to this abundance, in addition to the time to correspond, talk on the phone and meet, is that there's a sense that there is someone better just a mouse click away. If you are not desperate for a relationship, it is easy to reject every one, focusing on a fatal flaw. However, once in a while, when a guy seems to scratch a particular itch I'm feeling, I'll hang out with him for a while, until one of us realizes we aren't a good long-term match and it isn't fair to the other to continue as if we were.

So while abundance is a positive thing, when you find someone you click with, try to stay present to his good qualities, rather than thinking "Who else is online?" When I can see that my current man has been online within 24 hours of our being together, I know he doesn't think we're long-term either, even if neither of us says it.

You might just find an umbrella to fend off other potential suitors

So when it's raining men, come into the shelter of one guy and dry off for a while and see how it feels. Who knows, you might just find an umbrella to fend off other potential suitors — at least for a while.

Fresh out of men?

When you find yourself out of prospective dates, wouldn't it be great if you could just go to the store and pick up what you want? Would that it was that easy. In "Shopping for men" I described how sometimes you have to be creative and patient in your search.

An Adventures in Delicious Dating After 40 reader writes,

> *"What happens when you run out of men? I've been on two online dating sites for the last 2.5 years and feel like I see the same guys over and over. I've tried volunteering, asking friends, talking to men in the wine store. I'm about ready to give up. I'm just not finding anyone who floats my boat. Any thoughts?"*

I'm not really an expert on how to meet men, as nearly all my dates have come through online sites. But that doesn't stop me from having an opinion!

You're doing the right thing getting out there doing things you like and letting your friends know you're wanting to meet interesting men. You might expand even more by taking classes about things you want to know. I took a class in auto mechanics years ago, not to meet men, but to learn about my car. But there were some cuties in the class.

Also go to stores men frequent. As I say that, I realize you could probably meet a lot of men at the cigar store, but who could stand the smell? So don't go to places you don't have an interest in.

However, I make a point of looking presentable (not all dated up, but still clean and neat) when I go to the hardware and electronics stores. I've even asked attractive men for their opinions in both. While this hasn't yielded a date, you get used to talking to strangers, and you make sure you are presentable even for a Fry's run for CD-ROMs.

Someone once suggested that I take up golf as the ratio of men to women was in my favor! I took a golf lesson once and wasn't entranced, so I've ignored that advice. But for some women it would be perfect if they liked the game. There is a steady stream of men teeing up all day long!

Now, let's revisit the virtual part of your quest. When I've had dry spells in between men, I've adjusted my online activities. First, go back through those familiar faces and give them a little more focus. Sometimes I've found something in a guy's profile that sounds interesting beyond my initial first read. Or maybe he's posted a new pic that is more appealing that the previous one. If so, I make contact.

Second, if the site lists "mutual matches" or "reverse

matches" (as Match.com does), go through those to see if anyone new jumps out. Maybe one or two criteria kept them out of your original search, but it isn't really a deal breaker if he's 5-foot-eleven instead of 6-feet tall.

And third, try being a bit more liberal in your search criteria. For example, if your searches have been limited to 25 miles from your house, when you expand that to 50, many more matches will appear. The same with age, income, height, etc.

There are many more than two dating sites, so try posting your profile to others. Most don't require you to pay to post your profile, so you can see how much interest you get before you have to pony up and join.

Although I generally counsel women not to initiate the first contact, if you aren't getting a lot of emails, then time to take some action. In "Dear Fido" I share how I wrote to a guy's dog to make a fun first impression. And his dog wrote back!

A friend has had great success meeting interesting men through It's Just Lunch. Other introduction services like Table for Six can also offer new faces. If there's one near you and you aren't put off by the initiation fee, it can yield some great guys.

So if you're feeling you're running out of good prospects, either take a break from searching for a while, or mix up your efforts. Remember, just like shopping for clothes, shopping for men should be fun!

Safe online dating

A gal pal said she was afraid to date online because of safety issues. It's true that online you don't know much about the guy. But that is true if you meet him in a store, bar, on a singles hike or dance. So there are some precautions you take no matter where you meet someone, but especially with online connections.

💜 ***Set up an email address that doesn't include your name.*** You can set up free email accounts through Yahoo!, Google, Hotmail and others. Make sure you don't put your name in the "from," just your handle. The reason you don't want to put your name in the "from" is someone can easily Google you and in some cases, find out where you live or work, go to church, or frequent other places if there is a posting with your name on a web site. I've found out where guys worked and lived, complete with a map to both, by a little Google sleuthing.

💜 ***Only give your cell phone number.*** Did you know that someone can find your home address and map if you give them a listed landline number? So if you give him your number, only give your cell. And to be even safer, take his number but don't give him yours.

💚 ***Tell a friend where you'll be.*** Email your pal all the information you have on your date, his name, phone, address, work. Tell her where you're meeting him and a check-in time. If you don't call her within 10 minutes of that time, she is to start calling you and him.

💚 ***Only meet him in public places for the first few dates.*** When I've made exceptions to this rule, I've been sorry. Not because of safety concerns, but because it is harder to extricate yourself from an uncomfortable situation or send him home if things get too heated. So now I only meet him in a public place for the first few dates.

💚 ***Don't get in the car with him on the first date.*** He may seem fine at first, but you are totally at his mercy when you are in his car. Always take your own car, no matter how nice he seems. If he pressures you or tries to make you feel silly for wanting to have your own car, you know it's time to leave. Same with him wanting you to drive him somewhere. Don't do it, no matter how trustworthy he seems. Ninety-nine percent of the time it will be fine, but you don't want to worry about that 1 percent that creates a problem.

💚 ***Ask about him at places he frequents.*** I learned a potential suitor worked at a company where another friend worked. After we set up a lunch date, I called my friend. She said she thought he was married. She checked around and found out that yes, he was. I cancelled the date. Another guy attended the same Rotary as a friend of mine. I asked her about him and she said he was a good guy. Had she said anything negative, I would have re-thought if I wanted to meet him. If I did, at least I would know my friend's take on him.

Keep your guard up for the first few dates

While the above seem common sense, I've ignored each one. Now I don't. Not that I've been in any dangerous situations, but I've realized I could have been. So keep your guard up for the first few dates. Even after that, someone could turn out strange, but I find most guys are on their best behavior for the first few dates, then their true nature begins to come out. So don't make exceptions to the above until you are pretty confident he is a good guy.

Is 21st Century dating unnatural?

Speed dating. Internet dating. Meeting for the express purpose to see if there's a romantic spark.

Some people say this is unnatural. When we date this way, we base our decision to see each other again on very little information, mostly physical. Even after days, weeks, or months of emails, texts, IMs and calls, it can all fizzle if there's no physical spark.

In the "natural" way, you met someone through friends, work, class, the neighborhood, gym, church, etc. You had some interaction with him, usually over a period of time, and got to know him a bit. You were perhaps physically attracted to him, but you were also attracted to how he spoke, treated you and treated others. Once you went out you knew you were drawn to him at some level.

Some cultures take the picking entirely out of the couple's hands. Using matchmakers or arranged marriages, others decide who would be right for you. Many,

many of these marriages have not only been happy, but have lasted until one partner died. They learned to love each other, even if there was no initial spark.

While we know millions of people have met, fallen in love and established committed relationships through the new dating techniques, it doesn't work for a lot of people. However, if you live in a small town with limited age-appropriate singles, or work alone, or have family responsibilities that limit your social interaction, it may be hard to meet people the "natural" way. So you look to the "unnatural" ways to fill the void.

The Twenty-first Century methods, however, set up an awkwardness that isn't found in the older methods. On the first date you are evaluating: "Do I like his hair? His manner? His humor? His clothes? His conversation? Does he give and take in the discussion? Does he seem to take care of himself? Did he have too many drinks at dinner? Does he badmouth his ex?" The list is endless. Men do the same thing.

When meeting someone in the natural way, you are not in "date" mode. You're just hanging out, or doing some activity at the same time, perhaps jogging on the treadmill next to each other. If you enjoy each other's company, after a few times of this, one of you will suggest coffee afterwards. That may happen a few times before one of you suggests a movie, dinner, or other activity. You've grown fond of each other a bit before starting down the dating path. You're not evaluating him in the same way you are on a first virtually blind date.

Do you think today's new way of dating is better?

However, in the natural way, you don't necessarily know if he's married if he's not wearing a wedding ring. You don't know if he's in a relationship. And yes, although people can (and do) lie online about their relationship status, most tell the truth. People lie in person, too. If you met someone through a social circle, you can quickly check with others to see what they know about him. But even that is not always accurate, depending on what he's told them.

What do you think? Do you think today's new way of dating is better because you know more about a man than someone you met at a class or at the gym? What do you see as the advantages of the "natural" and "unnatural" ways of dating?

What do men look at in your profile?

A dating friend told me what he thinks men look for in women's profiles. First, your picture. If he likes your face, he'll look for one that shows your body. If he likes your body type, he'll read more. After body, he looks for height. Then he'll look at age and what the woman says she wants. If she wants kids or if she has little kids, my friend moves on.

He asked me what women look for. I told him what I look for, as I really can't say what other women look for. I first look at height, age, then at the photos. I look to see if he's got kids at home (not optimal for me), if he lives alone or with roommates (I'm not fond of room-mate situations), then how he expresses himself. If he is articulate and ideally funny, doesn't have more than a few typos, and has made the effort to write more than a few lines, I continue. I then look at education, although I've met some great guys who didn't graduate college. I also note occupation, income, and his lifestyle.

I read what he's looking for. If he wants someone younger, shorter and thinner than me, I know we're probably not a good match. However, if he's contacted me, I will respond if he sounds interesting.

"Could I make her happy?"

My friend told me that when men read profiles they are basically asking "Could I make her happy?" So if she has a jet-setting lifestyle and he's a couch potato, he passes. Or if she loves opera and the symphony and he's a hard rock guy, then he moves on. So when you write your profile, answer the question that's on the guys mind: "What does she want to make her happy?" Your writing will be more captivating that way.

Marketing 101 for dating

Today I was strolling down the fresh men aisle at my favorite dating site. No one was enticing enough to pick off the shelf and examine more closely. I wasn't even drawn to read any labels (profiles).

What was wrong?

Lack of marketing.

With very few exceptions, online daters don't know how to get people to pause and investigate their profiles. What stops eager shoppers from delving deeper?

1. ***Poor pictures.*** Blurry, dark, or the face is covered with sunglasses and/or a hat. I've covered this before in "Is that you? Pictures are just a rough facsimile of the real thing."

2. ***Bad title.*** Most sites allow you a few words to describe yourself in a title. I've seen titles that included "lonely," "horny," and "desperate." Don't you just want to write those guys immediately?

And there are the misspellings. My favorite is "intellegent" [sic] which shows up more than you'd think.

If the guy has a decent pic and headline, you read his profile. Many — even college graduates — have a difficult time here. I read one the other day that listed his history back to high school. Others tell you every outdoor activity in which they have ever participated. Some list so many sports they play, I get tired just reading about them. Others include hints at baggage: "No liars, cheaters, or gold diggers." "Not looking to be anyone's meal ticket." "Pass me by if you're a player." Can you tell he still has some work to do? And does he really think a player would say, "Oh, boy, I better pass on this guy." Right.

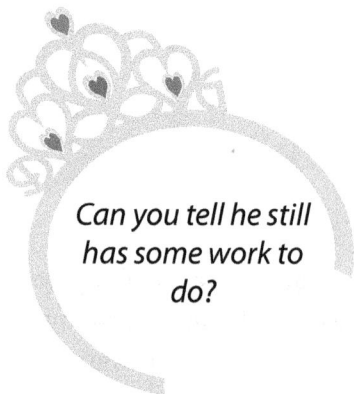

Can you tell he still has some work to do?

So how do you turn a boring profile into something more interesting? Here are three tips from Marketing 101.

♥ *Talk benefits.* Paint a picture of what life would be like with you. Don't just say "I'm fun" — give an example: "I have fun at most anything, and we can laugh our way through cooking dinner together, taking a twilight stroll, or picnicking on the beach." If you like outside activities, don't just

say, "I like tennis, biking, hiking, and kayaking."
Yawn. Try "We can explore the beauty of the area
while getting to know each other through hiking
the regional parks, kayaking on the lake, or biking along the river trail."

💜 *Use "you" not "he."* Put the "customer" into the
copy. So instead of saying "he" when describing
your ideal guy, say "you" so he can put himself
there with you.

💜 *Ask for the order.* "We should talk if..." or "If this
sounds like you, please email me a hello" or "If
you want to see if I'll laugh at your jokes, send
me an email." Something — almost anything
— that calls for action. Ads do this all the time:
"Call now" or "Reserve your space." There's a
reason they do this — it works!

Here's the before of a friend's profile, followed by
the revision after we worked on it:

Before

*I am a mature, well-educated professional female,
never married with no children. I have been told I
am rather witty and I enjoy a variety of activities
including reading, writing, painting, playing musical instruments, surfing the Web, managing my
online webstore, watching educational television,
drinking exotic coffees and having lively debates
with friends and family. I am politically liberal
with old fashioned moral values and am a bit*

quiet at first, but can be very talkative once you get to know me. I am a transplanted NYer, a tree hugger, a feminist, a humanist, an animal lover and a strong believer in the innate goodness of human nature.

I'm looking for: My ideal partner would be a well educated fellow professional with a big heart and a first rate sense of humor. Sensitivity and the ability to communicate freely and fully are very important to me, while treating others with dignity and respect is a must. A liberal political mindset is also an important asset. If you are a mature single, divorced or widowed man, preferably without children and are interested, please feel free to contact me. And always, always remember: we are all here for the chocolate!

After:

My man is a special guy. In addition to being a well-educated fellow professional, you have a big heart and a first rate sense of humor. You laugh easily, and especially at your own silliness as well as mine. Perhaps you are like me in that you giggle at small children's unselfconsciousness, or dogs playing, or odd typos in the paper. You pride yourself on your ability to communicate freely and fully and appreciate that I do, too. You wouldn't consider treating others with anything but dignity and respect. We share a liberal political mindset.

I've been told — by people other than my family — that I'm rather witty. Like you, no doubt, I enjoy a variety of activities including reading, writing, painting, playing musical instruments (but don't worry, not accordion), surfing the Web, managing my online webstore, watching educational television, drinking exotic coffees and having lively debates with friends and family. I'm politically liberal with old-fashioned moral values. I'm somewhat quiet at first, but converse freely once you get to know me. I am a transplanted NYer, a tree hugger, a feminist, a humanist, an animal lover and a strong believer in the innate goodness of human nature.

I'd prefer a man who doesn't have children at home, so if your daily dad duties are over, and the above fits you, we should talk!

And always, always remember: we are all here for the chocolate!

Try applying these ideas to your own online efforts.

Euphemisms uncovered

In dating profiles common phrases are used that are really euphemisms — nice ways to say what isn't totally true. While I know you'd never use any of these duplicitously, others do. Some of these I've learned the hard way, as I am generally trusting and believe people at their word. But I've found that some people have very different definitions of certain words. Let me share what I've learned certain words mean in the real world:

💙 passionate — horny

💙 handsome — my mama tells me this all the time so I must be

💙 fit — I can walk from my car to my office without getting too winded

💙 athletic — I played football (or some sport) in high school, but I haven't seen the inside of a gym or played a physical game — unless you count sex — since then

💙 chivalrous — I'll open the door for you, at least until we've had sex a few times

💙 intellegent (sic) — not

- funny — my fart jokes crack up my buddies

- gentlemanly — I won't attack you until the end of our first date

- separated — living in the same house with wife, sleeping in same bed, sometimes having sex, but not often enough so am listing myself on this dating site

- curvy — chubby

- voluptuous — obese

- a few pounds overweight — fat

- average build – 20-40 lbs. overweight

- Amazon — huge

- want to have fun — want to have sex

- looking for the one — looking for the one for right now until someone better comes along

- want a sensational friendship — friends with benefits

- tired of the bar scene — I can't even pick someone up when they are drunk

- romantic — horny

- adventurous — kinky

- give flowers for no reason — you'll be lucky if you ever see a daisy

- independent — stubborn as a mule

- quirky sense of humor — I'm so weird no one will date me

- like a drink — I sometimes forget where I live and the cops have to bring me home

- enjoy the finer things in life — you better be as rich as Bill Gates

- like mountain climbing, scuba diving, triathalons, skydiving – I like watching them on TV

- traditional values — you must treat me like a queen, and don't expect sex

- family values — if you're not ready to make babies, don't bother me

- must love dogs — you're going to be #2, at best!

- I only date beautiful women — I'm incredibly shallow. Lose your looks and I'm gone

What phrases or words in online profiles have you learned mean something entirely different than you expected?

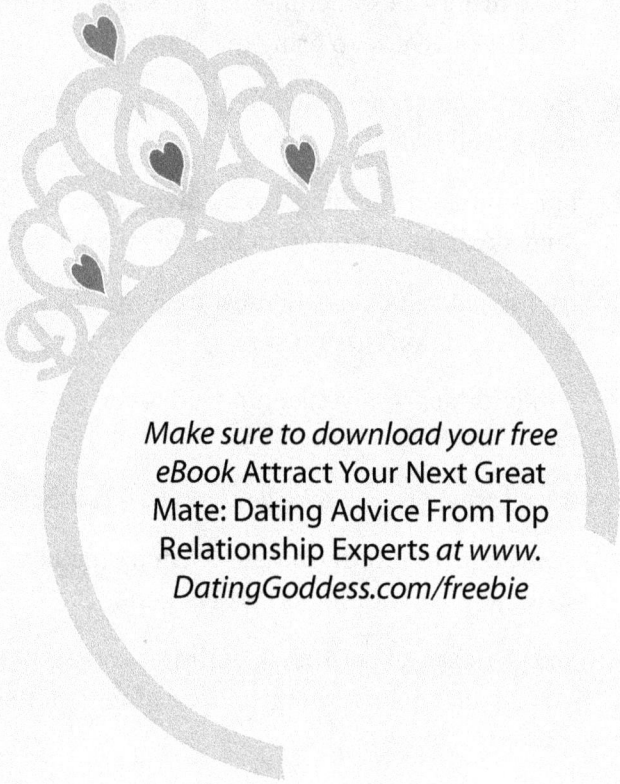

Make sure to download your free eBook Attract Your Next Great Mate: Dating Advice From Top Relationship Experts *at www. DatingGoddess.com/freebie*

Dating karma

I believe what goes around comes around. How you treat others is how you will be treated. Of course, there are always exceptions — you were cranky with someone and she went out of her way to be nice. Or you were nice, and he was mean. But generally, I believe if you are polite, thoughtful, and classy, that is what you will attract to you.

So I always make a point of thanking my dates, especially if he bought coffee, lunch or dinner. I would thank anyone who bought me a gift, so why not a date? I email him thanking him for meeting me and mentioning something I enjoyed from our conversation. If I'd like to see him again, I say so. If not, I tell him we're not a match. But I do so gently and kindly.

I think the most important time to keep focused on dating karma is during a break up. A guy I'd dated for six weeks recounted all my flaws during an email telling me

Keep focused on dating karma during a break up

why he was breaking up with me. I could have countered with an even longer list of his flaws, but I thought better of it. What would it do but let me vent, and why inflict that vitriol on anyone? Instead, I said, "You're right, we're not a match. I wish you the best. Goodbye." And I moved on.

When someone is mean to me I ask who do I want to be in response? Someone as low as him? No. I think better of me than he does of himself. So I work to be gracious and classy and move on.

Are you describing yourself compellingly?

"To say something nice about themselves, this is the hardest thing in the world for people to do." — Nancy Friday

If you are online dating, how do you describe yourself in your profile? Does it really reflect who you are? And if you're not online, you might consider writing a description of yourself and what you want, just for the practice. But be prepared to experience some frustration. Most people have trouble describing themselves compellingly.

My dating neighbor asked me to review her online profile and suggest any changes that would help her get more appropriate responses.

This is an amazing woman. In addition to being a top Stanford grad and a loving and patient mother of three teenagers, she is a top doctor who loves her work and patients. She is one of those special people who never flaunts her accomplishments or intelligence, and instead has a gentle demeanor, easy smile, and down-to-earth presence. She's fit, energetic, athletic, slender, and pretty. She looks ten years younger than her 48 years.

So how did this special woman describe herself in her profile? Pretty pedestrianly. She emphasized her girl-next-door characteristics and that was it. She didn't mention her profession, nor her enthusiasm for life.

> *This special woman described herself pedestrianly*

While I don't consider myself particularly gifted at writing other peoples' profiles, here's how I rewrote her description:

> *High-achieving gal-next-door wants to meet a similar nice guy.*
>
> *Do you love your life? I love mine. But I'd like to have that wonderful connection with a special man that fulfills each of our souls. Just like you, I have a full life already. Yet I know I want to invest the time to develop a relationship with someone special.*
>
> *My life involves a busy and fulfilling profession, three amazing teenagers, regular exercise, interesting travel, and extraordinary friends. I'm down to earth, with an easy smile and inquisitive mind.*
>
> *I'm looking for a man who is kind, thoughtful,*

intelligent, and has achieved his own successes and has a life of his own. He loves spirited conversation with someone who has thoughts of her own. He's looking for a partner, an equal, to share life with, whether that's travel, dining, theater, or just a quiet evening reading together or sitting in the hot tub.

If you'd like to explore if we might be a good match, please contact me.

Once you've written your self-description, run it by some friends, both male and female. The men will think you should include different things than the women. Listen to them!

The dating profile fudge factor

I may have led you astray.

In "You are (probably) more attractive than you think you are!," (in my book *Assessing Your Assets: Why You're A Great Catch*) I based my comments on the observation that most midlife women I know think of themselves as less attractive than others rate them. And men tend to overstate their attractiveness.

But a study reported in *Freakonomics: A Rogue Economist Explores the Hidden Side of Everything* sets my premise on its ear. The authors, Steven Levitt and Stephen Dubner, quote research* conducted by two economists and a psychologist who analyzed how 22,000 active online daters rated their appearance, among other things. They compared these findings to the national average to show that online daters exaggerate.

Are we surprised? No.

What is surprising is the amount of the embellishment.

Just like in Garrison Keillor's Lake Wobegon, where "the women are strong, the men are good looking, and all the children are above average," so too people describe themselves as exceptional in the online dating world. But this extraordinariness extends to the appearance of men *and* women — at least the single adults listing themselves on dating sites.

Seventy-two percent of the women claimed "above average" looks. Of these, 24% claimed "very good looks." Men were a tad more modest — 68% rated themselves as "above average," with 19% of those saying they had "very good looks." Are we to surmise that single people — at least those listed on dating sites — are better looking than the general population? While many singles go out of their way to have makeovers, lose weight, and work out, are we to believe that 19-24% of these 22,000 people are very good looking? Doubtful.

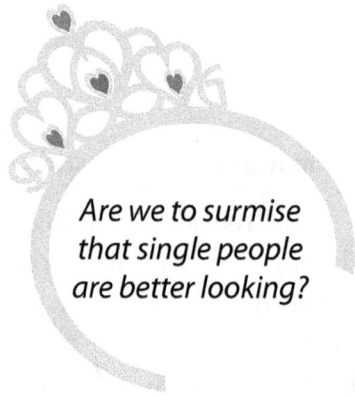

Are we to surmise that single people are better looking?

Only about 30% marked "average" in the appearance box, and 1% choose "less than average" looks.

So people are a bit delusional about how their looks compare to others, or they are concerned that if they put "average" no one will want to meet them. But isn't that what pictures are for?

Both genders listed heights averaging 1 inch taller than the national average. Men's weight was congruent with the national average, while women reported their weight as 20 pounds less than the national average. One can understand this as men are penalized for being short, and women for being fat. My experience is that most women wouldn't notice an inch of height on a man, and most men don't really know what women weigh, but they have a sense that women should weigh less than 125 pounds. They don't realize that sex symbols like Mariah Carey and Tyra Banks weigh 150-160, and that number sounds like someone who's fat.

The embellishment continues. Four percent of the online daters say they earn more than $200,000 a year, but only one percent of typical Internet users earn that much. Are successful people more likely to engage in online dating? Probably not. More of them are likely to use a matchmaker for a finding a partner. Are they greatly exaggerating? Yep.

So what do we make of this information? You have likely already figured out to take what people say in their profiles with a grain of salt. Last week I went out with a man who claimed to be 6-feet tall, but with my 2-inch heels on my 5-foot-10 frame I was at least an inch taller.

Are you justified in stretching the truth to get more responses? If you are like 21% of the women in the study and get no responses to your profile, you may be tempted to fudge — post a younger picture, shave off a few years, say you're slender when you carry 25 extra pounds. (BTW, the report didn't say how long the people in the study had been listed on the site. But for some perspective, 56% of the men didn't get one email.)

My advice: Don't fudge. Today I got a wink from a 53-year old man who admits to stating he's 51 in the demographics section in order to get more responses. Does he really think 2 years is going to make a big difference? However, duplicity does. What else might he be stretching the truth about? "Divorced" really means "separated" or worse "married in a loveless relationship but we stay together for the kids"?

* *"What Makes You Click? — Mate Preferences and Matching Outcomes in Online Dating"* by Gunter J. Hitsch, Ali Hortasu and Dan Ariely

Don't give your phone number too soon

In talking to a potential suitor, I learned that a woman should not give a man her phone number too quickly. When I asked why, he said, "It makes her seem too cavalier about it. I think she must give it to everyone this quickly, so I don't feel special. I'd rather wait until we've exchanged a few emails to see if we click."

He also shared that he hates it when a woman seems demanding when she gives her number and says "Call me." rather than inviting him to call with a more pleasant "I'd welcome a call." or "Please call if you'd like to chat." I typically use the latter, and only give my number after a few email exchanges.

"I'd welcome a call."

So even though you think it shows you're interested by giving your

number, wait a bit. He may ask for it, or give you his first. However, even if he does either, it does not necessarily show he's interested. One guy seemed interested and after a few email exchanges, gave me his number. I called him and didn't hear back. I waited a few weeks, sent him an email asking if he still wanted to connect. He said he did. I called him again. Nothing.

Next!

Do you tell suitors how to make you happy?

My friend Bruce says most women don't know how to express how a man can make her happy. Women commonly say they want nebulous characteristics, like successful, strong, communicative, fun. A woman's profile often says she wants a long list of nearly impossible attributes. A man begins to read the superman-like list and moves on, as he knows he can never measure up.

A man wants to make a woman happy. But he needs a clear roadmap. Do you like fresh-perked coffee in the morning? Sunset walks? Foot massages? He knows he can – or can't – provide what you want. He also wants to be able to make you happy without going far outside his regular activities. So if he's an outdoors guy and you say you like hiking and camping, he says, "I can make her happy taking her backpacking." If you say, "I like concerts," he says, "So do I! I'd like to take her to hear some great performers."

Now this may seem like common sense that a guy looks for women who like to do what he likes to do. But

I think it's more than that – it's all around his making you happy. If you say you like opera and he doesn't, he knows he could take you, but he won't be completely comfortable. He's willing to go to the opera every once in a while, but he'd be very happy if you'd be thrilled on the back of his Harley.

What makes you happy?

What makes you happy? Write it down. Based on Bruce's concept, I've rewritten my online profile. Following is how I've expressed what makes me happy. Maybe it will give you some ideas on how to say what you want.

If you are my man, you know you can make me happy — and I'll make you very happy. You're strong yet sensitive. You listen carefully first and make sure I feel heard before trying to fix anything.

You show your love through everyday actions: kind words, making me laugh, sharing a favorite last cookie, taking care of life's messy parts. You like to open jars, take out the garbage, bring in the groceries, ensure the cars have proper maintenance. You show your caring by planning special outings from picnics on the beach, to concerts, dinners, or plays. You plan romantic evenings at home by preparing a fire, lighting candles, playing soft music and clearing the sofa for cuddling.

You make me laugh at your silliness. You love talking about things that are important, not drivel. You know we needn't agree on everything, and we disagree respectfully.

You're chivalrous and regularly show me I'm special through many little acts like opening doors, pulling out chairs, helping with my coat.

You love to take me abroad, and when we travel, you like to make sure I'm taken care of. You make the arrangements and so we can relax and enjoy the journey together. You know I can do these things myself, but you know how much I appreciate it when you take care of it all.

You know I think you're sexy when you show pride in your appearance. While shorts, t-shirts and sweats are okay around the house, gym or on a hike, you wouldn't take me to the movies or dinner like that.

You are a generous lover, graciously receiving as well as giving. You know I like to dance, and we have a blast together. You're willing to try new things that you think we'd both enjoy.

You like to learn and grow spiritually, psychologically, and intellectually, and are always looking for ways to improve. You're happy with who you are, yet know you can get even better.

Write what a man can do to make you happy.

No, I will not be dating your Harley

I am often amazed at the pictures guys post in their profiles. After 3.5 years of online man shopping — looking at profiles — I shouldn't be surprised anymore. But based on all the pictures of men with their motorcycles, these must be babe magnets. I've even seen men post 12 pictures of their bike — with only one of themselves.

Men also post pictures of their cars — with or without themselves in the pic, and of course their boats and planes. This made sense when I realized they wanted to show the material trappings of their financial success. However, they could be up to their eyeballs in hock to pay for such toys. I'd be more impressed if they posted the first page of last year's tax return and a net worth statement!

"I'd welcome a call."

They also post pictures of their dogs, which I understand as most dog owners are very attached to their pets. However, sometimes there are more pics of the dogs than them.

And some like to post nature pictures, especially if they say they are outdoors types, which 90% say they are. I don't mind a pic of a favorite place, but again, often the guy isn't in the pic. Or if he is, he has on a t-shirt, sunglasses and a hat, so I can't really see what he looks like.

So, if you like motorcycle-riding guys — sort of the "bad boy" image even though he may be a dentist or accountant — you'll be in online-dating heaven. Just make sure he pays as much attention to you as he does to his bike.

Playing the online dating game

Sometimes someone makes a first contact online, you look at the profile and there's no picture. In fact, in place of the picture the dating site says "Ask for a picture."

One man's memorable profile says "I care whats [sic] inside not the cover and its important that the first thing her email says is not send me a picture (how shallow). I am not Robert Redford or Mel Gibson but I can hold my own when it comes to looks but this does not mean I am ready to send a photo to the world."

This guy clearly doesn't understand how the online dating game works. And good or bad, a photo says volumes about a person. It's not just whether you think he is attractive or not, it's what a person decides to post. A 53-year-old guy posted — as his only pic — one of him at 17. What is he thinking? Others post photos that are too dark to see his face, or too small, or in a dirty t-shirt, or with sunglasses and a hat. Obviously, all these guys are clueless about how the game is played.

Another clueless person was one who wrote me a nice email. I am not a member of the site, so I could only respond with the site's predetermined responses. Usually, when you write someone, you give your email in case s/he isn't a member. He did not. Then he wrote me a nasty email complaining that I'd only sent one of the predetermined messages. He didn't realize that if you aren't a member that's all you can send. I have joined sites just to respond to someone, but his response showed me how angry he can get over nothing, so I didn't want to join to write him. (See "Toad Rage on page 85.)

So you have to know how the game is played and play along. Trying to buck the system will only get you heartache — and few dates!

You have to know how the game is played

Pictures: To post or not to post — that is the question

A single friend was sharing the challenge of finding Mr. Right. In her early 40's, never married, educated, intelligent, funny and beautiful, she wants to have a family and is feeling the pressure.

When discussing online dating sites, she said she doesn't post her picture because she wants men to be attracted to her because of what she says in her profile, not what she looks like. She knows that it is easy to be swayed by looks and doesn't want to someone to be attracted just by her picture.

However, she isn't finding a steady stream of qualified men beating a path to her In Box. I understand her desire to find someone who is attracted to her for her values and life philosophy. However, her no-picture strategy isn't working for her.

To be successful in anything you have to continually evaluate if what you are doing is helping you get what you want. If not, you have to be willing to try something new. My friend would probably see a dramatic increase in contacts if she posted her picture. Yes, that means having many men contact her who aren't good prospects. But she would enlarge her pool dramatically and be able to choose to connect with those who met her criteria.

Are you sticking to something that isn't working because you're afraid to try something new? Just try it and see how the new strategy works. You can always go back to the old way if the new one is worse!

Is that you? Pictures are just a rough facsimile of the real thing

When I began online dating, I wouldn't respond to someone if their picture wasn't appealing, even if they sent an articulate, fun email. I also turned down any contact who I couldn't imagine kissing, based on his picture. I didn't meet a lot of new guys with these criteria!

Now I've learned that pictures in online dating profiles are an approximation of what the person looks like. Even recent photos don't reflect the twinkle in his eye, how cute he is when he smiles, or how he makes you laugh with that silly expression. So I've learned

Pictures are an approximation of what the person looks like

to give him the benefit of the doubt if his profile, emails and calls are intriguing.

The other rampant problem with photos is many folks (men and women, I'm told) post pictures more than five years old. I think it is dishonest to post any pics more than five years old, even if they are with recent ones, unless you put the date on them. I didn't recognize one guy when I met him because his pic was 10 years old. I was attracted to my first online date because of his picture with little kids. When I met him, I realized those were his now-grown kids, not the grandkids he'd mentioned to me. In other words, his picture was 30 years old!

I have also met lots of guys who posted pics from when they were 60 lbs. lighter, or had hair (or hair another color but gray). I understand they think that if they present themselves as younger, they will get more responses. Perhaps they expect they will use their charm to overcome the disappointment of their date when she is having coffee with the white-haired guy with the paunch, not the buff stud in the pic (from 20 years ago). It's seldom worked for me.

So, the lessons:

1)   Only post or send pics fewer than five years old, and

2)   If other things are compelling, go ahead and meet the guy even if his pic isn't.

Scantily clothed pictures

A gal pal new to online dating asked me:

"What does it mean when a man offers to send you scantily clad pictures, and you haven't even talked to him on the phone yet, let alone met?"

"Sex."

"Say more."

"When people want to exchange nearly nude — or even nude — pictures, I've found it means they are looking for sex, not a relationship. It's common among that crowd to exchange nude pictures — sometimes just shots of key parts! Since they are only looking for intimate encounters, it really doesn't matter what the rest of you looks like. They just want to make sure the equipment is to their liking."

"No!"

"Yep. One friend showed me a site where people post nude pics with their face cropped off."

"Amazing."

"Where did you meet this guy?"

"Yahoo Personals."

"This is a bit unusual for a YP contact, but not unexpected. There are other sites that cater to sexual hookups."

"This guy also asked if I had 'additional pics' to share, even though I have 8 posted on the site."

"He was wanting nude shots, and wanted to see if you'd know what he was talking about."

"So should I continue to communicate with this guy?"

"Only if you are looking for a sex-only encounter. By the way, I've also had men ask me my bra size in the second email, and one sent me a list of questions he wanted me to answer, including intimate details. So these guys let their intentions be known early on, even if they aren't explicit in their profile saying they want a sex-only encounter."

Have you experienced inquiries from men who got too intimate too soon? How did you deal with them?

Judging a guy by how well he ... punctuates

My friend Jeff Rubin (The Newsletter Guy) and I were chatting about dating profiles and punctuation. "Punctuation?" you ask. "That's a weird topic." Not to Jeff. You see, Jeff started National Punctuation Day (Sept. 24) to call attention to the importance of proper punctuation. The book *Eats, Shoots & Leaves: The Zero Tolerance Approach to Punctuation* helped garner a lot of attention to this topic.

I told Jeff I was drawn to men's profiles that were articulate, humorous and with proper spelling, grammar and — you guessed it — punctuation. Recently, I responded to a guy out of my geographical range because he said he was a "down-to-earth guy" — punctuated properly. Of course, he also met my other criteria, but it is so rare to see correct punctuation I swooned. Too bad our face-to-face date didn't end in an exclamation point!

Here's an example of a far-too-common profile writing style:

my dogs not helping!

dependable, loving, affectionate, communicative, low maintenance, lover of traveling,sweet, outdoorsy camper ,playful, great kisser, fetcher funny,cuddler,OOPS all thats my dog! oh well, like dog.. like owner! of course im the cuter one. seeking the same and more!

Do you find all those misspellings, bad punctuation and missing capitals appealing? I don't. I guess some people don't understand how important a first impression is.

After going out with a guy once, I had to tell him we weren't a match. He was good humored about it and teased me about why. I responded half kiddingly "It's because you write 'your' when you mean 'you're.'" Other common examples are using "it's" (it is) when "its" (possessive form) is what is called for. More than one man describes himself as "Intellegent" (sic) in his profile.

I know, you're thinking, "That's kinda shallow, isn't it? To judge someone on their punctuation?" It's only one piece of the puzzle. So be mindful of your own punctuation. When in doubt, go to the National Punctuation Day site where Jeff has a primer on proper punctuation and some terrific photos and products, www.NationalPunctuationDay.com.

Tips for initiating online contact

An Adventures in Delicious Dating After 40 reader asked:

> *Do you have any tips on initiating online contact in a way that will get someone's attention without sending them running for the hills? I've tried commenting on common interests or similar life situations with little success. In the last 3 weeks I've contacted 6 potential dates and had one response, who said he was seeing someone.*
>
> *What are some things to avoid when making contact with a hot prospect? I'm looking for men in the same age range, comparable level of activity and attractiveness. I must be missing something.*
>
> *What are your suggestions for online pictures? Most seem to be digital self portraits.*

I don't claim to be an expert in this, but let me share my observations.

Generally, my experience is it's nearly futile to initiate contact (See "Don't initiate"). I know, it sounds antiquated for an assertive, confident woman to not use these attributes in the online world. I'm just reporting my findings: when I've initiated, very few men have responded, and those who did didn't last past a coffee date even if I was interested in more. All of the men with whom I've had second dates and beyond have initiated contact. Perhaps our men readers can illuminate why this might be, as I can only speculate.

That said, when I do decide to make contact, here are some of my strategies.

Make an initial email short, upbeat, and comment on items he mentions in his profile that you found interesting or you have in common. If he's got the trite "I like sunsets, dining out, and chilling at home," I don't say I, too, like what 90% of every profile states. (In fact, if he's that cliched, I probably won't be drawn to him in the first place.)

The key is to not be too short, e.g., "You're cute. Call me." But also don't get verbose telling him all the reasons you think you're a match. If you have a humorous personality, let it shine through and be sure to add the smiley emoticon so there's no confusion that you're trying to be funny, not whacked.

I've also learned from the men I've gone out with that many find it a turn off to be told to call you, and they don't want you offering your number too soon. In "Don't give your phone number too soon" (see page 39)

I share that guys have said they want to be invited to call after the second, third or fourth email. So don't give it on the first email or you'll appear desperate or easy.

You'll only hear back from 10% of those you contact

I have a standard email template that I adapt to the individual. You don't want to spend too much time crafting a specific email as you'll only hear back from 10% of those you contact. I figure they don't respond because they are:

1)   uninterested and don't know how to say that nicely,

2)   are involved with someone,

3)   aren't a member of the site so can't respond without joining.

Whatever the reason, don't take it personally and just move on. If you want to try again in a few weeks, you can, just don't give it more than twice or you'll seem desperate or like a stalker. For the second email, see "Use funny emails for unresponsive contacts" (page 77) for one approach.

Even following these guidelines, you'll still only hear back from 1 in 10 contacts — if that. It is somewhat of a numbers game.

In terms of photos, I always scratch my head when

I look at men's profile pics. All but a few are too small, too dark, out of focus, over 5 years old, or with a hat and sunglasses, not showing the guy's face. Please, no self-portraits taken at arm's length or in a mirror. That screams that you don't have at least one friend who is willing to take a picture of you in a suitable surrounding when you're dressed presentably and in good lighting.

I suggest having a professional photo taken, but not a glamour shot. You don't want to have professional hair, make up, lighting, and Photoshopping if you rarely look that way. You want to present yourself at your best, but also how you are likely to look when he meets you. One of the most pervasive complaints about online dating is that people don't look at all like their pictures. (See "Is that you? Pictures are just a rough facsimile of the real thing," page 51)

Have a professional photo taken, but not a glamour shot

I recommend posting several photos, some in casual settings, some in more professional attire, and one or two in formal togs. Make sure you choose ones that show your attractiveness, not whatever you happen to have around. Also, avoid showing too much skin, as men interpret that as you are easy.

My friend Rachel Sarah, author of *Single Mom Seeking* recently said in her blog that single moms should avoid posting pics with their kids because there have been some psychos who get to the kids through dating the mom. Ugh! Generally, I think it's probably a good idea to not post pics of your kids anyway.

And no matter how much you love your favorite location, too many pics of landscapes make me wonder if the person doesn't want to show their own face. One or two is okay, as is one of your pet, but if there are too many pics without you in them, it makes me wonder. And please, please, please don't post photos over 5 years old, ideally within the last 3 years. No one wants to think they are showing up for the 25-year-old babe who now is 50.

For those who feel they've had more than 10% success in initiating contact, what can you share that works?

Make sure to download your free eBook Attract Your Next Great Mate: Dating Advice From Top Relationship Experts *at www. DatingGoddess.com/freebie*

Be creative to get his attention!

Last week I had two sublime dates, Wednesday and Thursday, with a new guy. I loved being with him, and from all he said and did, it seemed he felt similarly. He called twice Friday while on a business trip. He'd said it was fine to call him, so I left him a voice mail Sunday night, and he called Monday. Tuesday he sent two brief emails. Then nothing for nearly 3 days.

I'm used to guys calling or emailing every day, especially if it seems like there's a mutual attraction. Perhaps I was impatient. In the unstable first few weeks of a potential relationship, there is uncertainty. I was wanting some sign he was still interested. Call it insecurity. I try to rein it in, but unfortunately it leaks out despite my best attempts.

I didn't want to call him again — it seemed so desperate. After all, in *He's Just Not That Into You* it says guys don't like to be chased, and they will call if they are thinking about you and want to talk to you. So I decided to get creative.

Since he interviews and hires people as part of his job, I decided to write an email speaking his language.

Subject: Job application status request

Dear Dr. XX:

As you know, I applied for your organization's position of "sweetheart trainee" last week. I enjoyed very much our two interviews and thought I fit the job qualifications very well. You are a great interviewer! I thought the practice session Thursday night went particularly well, and I could see myself enjoying the job very much. From your response, it appeared that your needs and my skills were a fit.

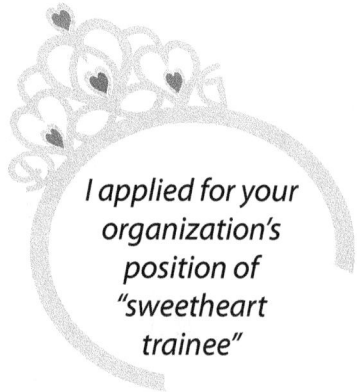

> I applied for your organization's position of "sweetheart trainee"

Since it's been a little while since we've touched base, I'm wondering if the position is still available or if it has been filled. Or perhaps you are still searching for a better-qualified candidate. I'm happy to have a third interview to determine if we are a good fit, before starting a probationary period.

I know you have been very busy with your frequent travel. But if you would be so kind as to tell me if the position is still available and if so, if

*I'm being considered for it, or if I should move on
to the next opportunity. I would love to fill the job,
and would be very sad if I'm out of the running, but
understand if you think it may not be a good fit.*

☺

An hour later he called laughing, as he'd just read
it. He said a coworker next to him wondered what was
so funny that caused him to laugh so loudly. I was glad
to hear from him. He apologized for not being in more
regular contact, that he'd work on being better, especially when he was traveling. We set a date for this weekend. Creativity can work!

Dear Fido

This guy kept coming to the top of my matches on one of the dating sites, so after a few months I decided to initiate contact, something I rarely do. This time, however, I decided to be creative.

I wrote to his dog mentioned in his profile, which we'll call "Fido" to protect his — and his owner's — identity.

Dear Fido:

You are cute! However I hope I don't offend you, but I think that guy you live with is even cuter. While I hope I get a chance to meet you and appreciate your sense of humor, I already appreciate his.

I'm writing to you to see if you can give me the real scoop, as he seems like a guy I'd like to get to know. Is he really as intelligent and funny as he appears in his profile? Or is that hyperbole to entice ladies to meet with him?

We enjoy some of the same things: hiking, biking, I've even done some scuba. I, too, am educated and well-traveled, and, like him, I love learning.

So, give me the skinny. What is he really like? He keeps showing up in my matches, so do you think we'd be a good match? If so, can you put in a good word for me when he's especially susceptible, like when you're snuggled up with your head on him and looking at him with those big eyes of yours? If you give me the inside scoop I promise to brush you and give you lots of treats. What do you say?

_____

(Fido's response)

Hi Goddess!

Sorry for taking so long to get back to you but I had to show your letter to my dad since I am not yet two years old and he doesn't like me to write to older women. He looked at your profile and said that you looked safe. He looked at your note to me and said that

> *If you give me the inside scoop I promise to brush you and give you lots of treats.*

you are obviously creative and funny. He looked at your picture and said that you are very pretty. He then wanted to write to you himself but I reminded him that your letter was to me, *not him.*

Well, if you go out with him and mind very well, you can look forward to having your ears scratched and your side rubbed until your leg kicks. And, if you climb up in his lap, he will love you up until you go to sleep.

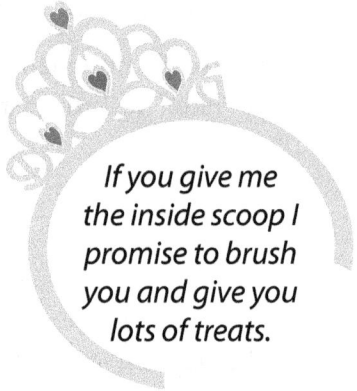

My dad was always very supportive when I was growing up. For example, he wanted me to get a good business education, so he spread out the Wall Street Journal on the kitchen floor for me to read when I was a pup. I remember getting too agitated over some of the articles and making statements on them before he got home. I guess I'm just a Blue State kind of dog. I even learned some French this way, but my dad says that my pronunciation suffers a bit, given my focus in life. For example, before each meal I say, "Bone appetite" and he says that's close but not really right. What do you think?

Do you have a dog for me to play with? Both my dad and I like playmates that don't growl or bite and don't arch their back and seem mean. We both like friends that like to run and play and go to the bathroom before we get in the car. I don't think he likes friends that drool on the side of the car when they hang their heads out the window either. I don't know how you two would ever figure out if you like each other since my dad says it's not polite to sniff. I just think it makes sense since I can find out if my friend is really a girl, is hot to trot, where she's been and what she's eaten.

Maybe you two should get a good rubber toy and play tug of war and chase each other. It works for me. If you would like to actually talk with me, you can call me at XX. My dad may answer if I'm sleeping but that's OK because then you can talk with him.

Fido (the hound of renown)

Dearest Fido, hound of renown:

Thank you for writing. Since it had taken awhile, I thought perhaps I had been too forward, or that your dad had found another (prettier, sexier, thinner, smarter, funnier) woman. I'm glad that you don't think that's the case. And you would know, wouldn't you?

<I am not yet two years old and he doesn't like me to write to older women.>

He is wise.

<He then wanted to write to you himself but I reminded him that you letter was to me, not him.>

He is welcomed to write himself. But I am glad you took the time to compose such a great letter.

<If you mind very well, you can look forward to having your ears scratched and your side rubbed until your leg kicks. And, if you climb up in his lap, he will love you up until you go to sleep.>

Yum! I will work very hard to mind if those are my rewards! Although I haven't been as well trained as you obviously have, so I hope there's no hitting with the newspaper if I misbehave. Sometimes I'm at my best when I'm misbehaving! Usually a look or stern voice are enough for me to see the error of my ways.

<"Bone Appetite".>

You are a very funny dog! I think I would cherish any dog who tries to speak French, no matter the pronunciation. If you will forgive mine, I will accept yours.

<Do you have a dog for me to play with?>

I'm sorry, I don't. But this is good, because I can lavish my pent-up dog affection totally on you! I am very affectionate (without being clingy), so I will welcome the opportunity to pet, brush, play with and cuddle you. Perhaps a little will rub off onto Dad. ☺

<Both my Dad and I like playmates that don't growl or bite and don't arch their back and seem mean. We both like friends that like to run and play and go to the bathroom before we get in the car. I don't think he likes friends that drool on the side of the car when they hang their heads out the window either.>

I would cherish any dog who tries to speak French

I think I qualify on all accounts.

I would like to talk to you both. However, Fido, what is Dad's name in case he answers the phone? I know I can always ask for you, but he might have to interpret until I can communicate with you face-to-face.

Goddess

———————

(After the first phone conversation)

Dearest Fido:

So we're meeting for coffee. I'm not sure if you'll be accompanying him or not. If not, I will have to meet you next time (assuming I'm not odious to him and there is a next time). Perhaps you can come to my house and chase some squirrels. You do like to chase squirrels, don't you? My back yard is infested with them and if you'd like to make your presence known and scare them off, I'd be grateful (read: more treats and brushing for you).

I did, however, have to practically pry his name out of him! I thought it a bit awkward to keep calling him Fido's dad, and I thought shortening it to just "Dad" was a bit presumptuous on a first conversation. He is hilarious, but you already know that. I think making each other laugh is key to a good relationship. I know, I know, you think a good walk, treats, and brushing are key. They are, I agree, for both dogs and humans.

Hey, he says one of his favorite books is *The House at Pooh Corner!* That cracked me up because for years when someone asked my favorite book, I cited that one! Wow! I've never met another adult who admitted to that in public! Cool! (I know, there were way too many exclamation points in that paragraph, but I was just excited. I'm calmer now. See, just periods.)

I hope to meet you soon. And thanks again for putting in the good word.

Goddess

————————

(Fido's response)

Whoof!!!

(To our coffee meeting, I took some dog treats, a *Winnie the Pooh* book and some fresh-baked home-made blueberry muffins, which I'd learned was one of Fido's dad's favorite foods.)

Goddess:

Thanks again for meeting me today. I really enjoyed getting to know you. I also appreciated your thoughtfulness in bringing the book and treats. The bagged [dog] treats were especially good and were very much like scones and very tasty with tea.

Fido's Dad

Hi Fido's Dad:

<Thanks again for meeting me today. I really enjoyed getting to know you.>

Me, too. But then I've always been a sucker for intelligent, good-looking, Winnie-the-Pooh-loving guys who own Dobermans, like blueberry muffins, have a quick wit and make me laugh.

<I also appreciated your thoughtfulness in bringing the book and treats.>

It just felt like the thing to do to thank Fido for his yenta services.

Goddess

_____

(The rest of the story: Although this exchange was fun and flirty, as was our meeting, I never heard from him again. So instead of thinking this creative writing was a waste of time, I look at it as a fun exercise.)

Don't initiate

A friend observed that dating for woman over 40 was different than for women under 40 because of the mixed expectations. Many midlife women have had career success because of their assertiveness — perhaps even aggressiveness. While that serves them in work, men don't typically want an aggressive woman in their personal lives.

However, my friend continued, younger women are expected to be aggressive in both parts of their lives. He believes younger men expect and accept that in a romantic partner.

> *In my personal life I have a do-not-initiate policy.*

I think it's difficult for most over-40 women to compartmentalize their lives and behavior to be aggressive at work but not in dating. While I have been successful in business by initiating contact with potential clients, in my personal life I have a do-not-initiate policy.

With few exceptions, I don't send the first email. I also ***never*** initiate the first date. I wait for the man to say "Shall we get together?" If he is not interested or assertive enough to ask, we aren't a good match. One man talked to me several times a week for a month and never asked me out. Finally, I told him we weren't a match.

While dating sites encourage you to make the first move, 90% of the men I contacted first either didn't respond or said they weren't interested. The few who responded positively ended up not being good matches.

Most men still want to be the pursuer. After the relationship has begun, it's usually OK to call him, or suggest an activity. But let him take the lead. If he doesn't, he isn't a match.

Use funny emails for unresponsive contacts

It is frustrating when you initiate contact with a guy you think is a good match, and you don't hear back. My single male friends tell me it's often because they don't feel it's a good match and they don't want to hurt your feelings by saying this, so they don't respond. Other pals have shared that some are involved with someone, but don't want to cut you off in case it doesn't work out with their current squeeze. So you feel like your email went into the same place lost socks in the washer go.

Occasionally, I'll be interested enough in a guy to follow up. I know I'm flattered when someone checks back a month or so later (recently a guy reconnected a year after the initial email, though we never met). So I devised this email to send and hopefully pique the unresponsive guy's interest enough to respond.

I sent you an email about a month ago, so am guessing that you (pick all that apply):

❏ *Didn't get it*

☐   *Got it but ignored it*

☐   *Got it but didn't find my profile intriguing*

☐   *Got kidnapped by aliens — again!*

☐   *Decided we live too far from each other and the thought of being far away from each other is un-endurable*

☐   *Broke your fingers while trying to karate-chop a wood plank so now can't type*

☐   *Found the love of your life*

☐   *Are too shy to respond to a woman emailing you*

☐   *Mom won't let me talk to strange women*

☐   *Were too busy to even consider dating*

☐   *Got offered a movie role and have been rehearsing love scenes with Cameron Diaz for oh so many hours*

☐   *Won the lottery and have now moved to a Pacific island*

☐   *None of the above and it's none of your business what I've been doing!*

I thought I should just check in with you.

A few have responded to my humor and creativity. Try it yourself and see what happens.

Have a good memory to avoid repeating mistakes

A nice-looking man emailed me. Based on his profile, he would be someone I would be interested in getting to know. He met most of my criteria.

However, as I looked at his picture, I felt I had seen it before. Had he appeared in my matches before? If so, he was such a good match, I would have made an exception to my "don't initiate" rule and contacted him. Had I done that? My cloudy memory seemed to remember some contact, but it went nowhere. Did he not respond? Say he wasn't interested?

I responded to his email asking if he remembered if we'd connected in the past. He said he didn't think so, and did I want to get together. Whoa, cowboy! He was moving too fast! On the second email wanting a meeting without even having a "get to know you a bit" phone call? Something was off.

Then I remembered. We had a phone call six months ago. I thought it was odd that he asked "If you felt the chemistry was right, how soon would you feel comfortable being intimate? The first date?" "No." "The second date?" "No." "The third date?" "I doubt it, but it is so dependent on how we click."

Although my radar was up that he was only looking for a quick roll in the hay, I agreed to meet him for coffee the next day. I tend to give people the benefit of a doubt, so I thought I may have misinterpreted his questioning. I took his cell number and he took mine.

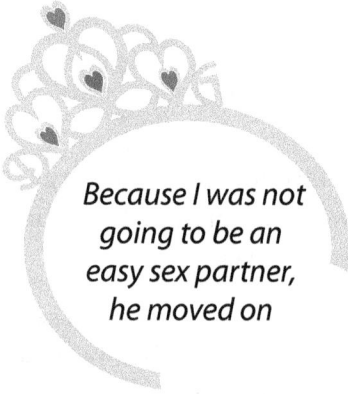

Because I was not going to be an easy sex partner, he moved on

I arrived at the coffee shop at the appointed time. I waited. And waited. And waited. After 20 minutes, I called his cell. Wrong number. Had I written it wrong or had he given me a fake number? I returned home. I emailed him asking what happened, giving him the grace of allowing he might have had an emergency. I never heard back.

I figured that because I was not going to be an easy sex partner, he moved on and stood me up without the decency to call and cancel. And now he was again wanting to meet me.

No, I will not be getting together with this inconsiderate guy. My memory is too good.

Online dating time equivalent to dog years

Sometimes you hit it off with someone online and you exchange a flurry of emails. That is if you ignore the advice in *The Rules for Online Dating*. Authors Ellen Fein and Sherrie Schneide tell women never to respond to an email from a potential suitor before 24 hours pass.

Well, I've ignored *The Rules*. But I've gotten to know guys quicker because of it. When you are exchanging several emails a day, someone's personality emerges much sooner than the weeks it would take if you followed Fein and Schneide's advice.

I liken it to the accelerated time passing of dog years. Depending on how quickly both of you respond, you can exchange numerous emails in a short period. One man even noted, "I don't interpret a prompt response to my emails as desperation, just interest." Fein and Schneide, however, say it makes you appear too eager.

IMs are even more lightning fast, as you are talking real time. You write something and he writes back almost immediately. I've grown fond of someone pretty quickly through IMs.

There's something about online communication that enables you to ask questions you may not if you are talking on the phone. Somehow it can seem easier admitting to insecurities and sharing histories, goals, dreams and baggage. Of course, you can do this on the phone and in person, but there's something akin to the anonymity of a confessional that lets people be forthcoming online. (Of course, there are always those who lie online, just as they would in person.)

Is all this warp-speed courting good? I'm not sure. I like getting to know someone quickly to see if any deal breakers emerge. Better than spending months to uncover the same problems. But the downside is a seeming intimacy that hasn't had time to really develop.

Toad rage

I don't label any of the men I've gone out with as losers, frogs, toads, jerks, freaks, geeks, dweebs, nerds or cads.

However, every once in a while, I come in contact with someone who acts immaturely — or toadlike. This was the case with a man who emailed me but didn't really understand the dating site's process. He got angry over something he didn't understand and blamed me.

He initiated contact with a short but specific email addressing some items in my profile. I responded promptly, but because I wasn't a member of the site, I could only use one of the predetermined responses the site provides.

He didn't understand that non-members can only respond with these brief pre-written lines, so his response to me was:

> *"I really hope you can come up with more than a coppied [sic] message. I don't mean to be rude but I'm a person who puts alot [sic] of effort into communicating and I feel slighted when others don't put effort into a response.*
>
> *"Respectfully Yours"*

Well, this doesn't sound very respectful, does it? These two sentences told me a lot about this man.

1. He didn't understand the site. If you are new to a site, you may not really know how it works, so I can give him some slack on this.

2. He assumed I was lazy or rude. He jumped to a conclusion based on minimal information. Instead of saying something like "Thanks for your positive response. I hope to hear more from you in the future," he lambasted me. Is this a way to try to start a relationship? I don't think so.

    He assumed I was lazy or rude

3. For someone "who puts alot [sic] of effort into communicating" he didn't put enough effort into proofreading before hitting the send button. C'mon — it's only two sentences, not a treatise. How hard is that to check for spelling errors?

4. He seemed to get angry over a tiny thing. If something like this sets him off, what would life be like around him? Would he yell at inconsiderate drivers, slow waiters, inattentive clerks? Is that the kind of guy I'd want to spend time with?

No.

So while he made some assumptions about me based on my predetermined response, I, too, made some decisions about him as well.

I've learned that you really can tell a lot about someone by their initial emails, phone calls and first dates. Yes, give him a little slack, but if his comments and behaviors show anger over inconsequential things, best to move on. You don't want to be the recipient of toad rage.

Virtually falling for a guy

I mean "virtually" two ways:

1. As the dictionary defines it: "nearly, almost" as in not really; and

2. Via the computer and/or phone; not face to face.

A friend and I were once again comparing dating notes. She's dipped her toe in the dating water a bit the last six months, going out with a handful of men. Currently, she is emailing two men she met through Chemistry.com. Both are interesting, intelligent, witty, and engaging. She finds the email veil allows her to get to know their personalities without the distraction of determining if she is physically attracted to either one.

However, while it is important to enjoy getting to know how a guy thinks and communicates — at least in writing — we all know that it takes more than discourse to create a love interest.

I have fallen for guys because of their emails or

then through their phone calls only to have the attraction dissipate when meeting face to face. Sometimes it is my not finding them appealing, or they have irritating habits that quickly surface. Or they are not drawn to me, or I have some twitch that sends them packing.

A Kansas-based friend communicated with a man in Scotland via email and ,nightly hour-long VOIP conversations. They frequently sent care packages to each other. After six months, he took two weeks vacation to come meet her. Because of his limited funds, he asked if he could crash on her couch in the small 2-bedroom, 1-bath house she shared with her two daughters.

I've fallen for guys virtually only to have the attraction dissipate

Although they had exchanged pictures, of course the 3-dimensional person looked different than either expected. But because they had built up a bond through the ether, they were at least not repulsed. However, as each day of his visit progressed, she became less and less enamored with him. Since this 38-year-old man lived with his parents, he didn't bother to pick up his wet towels from her bathroom floor, nor help with any dinner preparation or clean up. After dinner, his rear became wedged in her recliner while she and the girls cleaned up. Other irritating, self-absorbed habits quick-

ly emerged so she was ready to send him packing in less than a week. The "real" Scot was quite different than the "virtual" one.

If he isn't in person as you'd hoped, it's easy to think that all the time you spent communicating with a guy is wasted. Perhaps you are honest and say, "I've really liked how we communicated these last few weeks, but I'm not feeling the spark to think we have a romantic connection. Would you be willing for us to remain in contact as friends?" Many men see this as the kiss of death and may say "yes" but not initiate nor respond to any contact in the future.

During those weeks of emailing, you have, no doubt, enjoyed yourself, so it was a form of entertainment. And you may have learned something about yourself as you responded to his questions. Maybe he asked, "Who do you think the best US president was?" and you hadn't really thought about it. You spend a little time ruminating before you respond, then are pleased with your answer and supporting arguments. You've uncovered something you didn't know about yourself!

And of course, maybe he'll accept your invitation — or offer his own — to be your pal. I keep in touch with over a dozen guys I went out with who are now my pals and I treasure each of them. So even if you have the attitude that you don't need any more friends, don't totally discard an interesting guy so quickly, even if there is no romantic spark. And you never know when a romantic spark may be kindled once you get to know each other's hearts better.

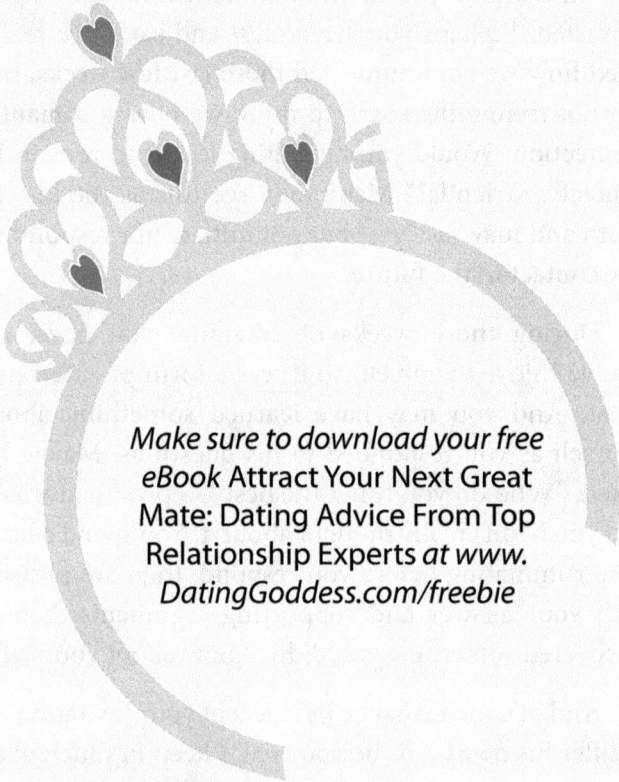

Make sure to download your free eBook Attract Your Next Great Mate: Dating Advice From Top Relationship Experts at www. DatingGoddess.com/freebie

Pass on no-effort guy

I broke my own rule the other day — I initiated contact with a guy. I don't know why I do this — the results are almost laughably predictable. He had looked at my profile but didn't write. I thought he was cute, smart, articulate, so I wrote.

His response: "I live close to [intersection about 10 miles from me]. If you ever find yourself coming to this area maybe we can plan a chance meeting."

Translated: "I don't have much desire to meet you and am not willing to make any effort, so if you come to me, I'll eke out a few minutes to deign to see if you have any appeal to me."

"I'll eke out a few minutes to deign to see if you have any appeal to me."

Well, buddy, your inertia is unappealing. Even if we lived a ways apart, you could at least offer to meet half way if you're so lethargic that you can't muster the extra 5 miles to meet near me, which most guys do.

And, by the way, how does one "plan a chance meeting"? It's an oxymoron. That's like planned spontaneity. You can't plan a "chance" meeting.

So, no, pal, I won't be calling you nor driving to your neighborhood for that planned chance meeting.

When will I learn that if they don't initiate they have no energy for you?

Should you respond to someone about whom you're ambivalent?

Y ou receive a nice, personalized email from a man on a dating site. He's crafted an message specific to you, commenting on items from your profile. His profile is fine, but something is a borderline deal breaker. You vacillate whether to respond with your nice boilerplate "Thanks but no thanks" email, or to encourage more interaction.

No doubt like you, I've received lots of contacts from guys who clearly weren't a fit, or of enough interest for me to meet for coffee. Those were easy to deal with. I simply sent them my "Thanks but no thanks" email.

The slippery slope begins when you have ambivalence but decide to write back anyway. There was nothing odious about his profile or communication, but also nothing really compelling. And there was that one (or more) issue that raised a yellow flag. Not to say this is always bad, as I've met some great guys who I initially thought weren't of interest, some of whom I dated multiple times or others who became beaus.

But more often than not, I knew we weren't a match from the get go. However, his email was so nice, or he was articulate, or there was something interesting in his profile to offset the borderline deal breaker. So I answered the email, which progressed to a phone call, which led to coffee. And after you've built a bit of a bond through multiple emails and phone calls, when you meet and there's no spark, it's uncomfortable to have to tell him so.

In "Hello — goodbye: How to say 'no thanks' after meeting" (in the *Moving On Gracefully: Break Up Without Heartache* book), I discussed how to gently yet clearly let a guy know you aren't a match. I always feel badly when I must have that conversation when I was pretty sure we wouldn't be a match from the beginning.

"Why even encourage him?"

"Then why even encourage him?" you rightly wonder. Because some of my most special guys were ones who I was close to emailing a "no thanks" message. But after some emails, phone calls and coffee, I warmed to them. In "'I only want to date someone I would marry'" (in the *Assessing Your Assets: Why You're A Great Catch* book) I shared that as long as there aren't glaring red lights and he seems interesting, go ahead and meet for coffee.

Sometimes you respond to his initial email out of selfishness. You haven't had a date, let alone an interesting, flirty email conversation in a while. Maybe you are lonely. Or bored. And there's no one else on the horizon. He seems nice enough, so who knows? So you respond, even though you're 90% sure you're not a good match. That's not really a good way to start any relationship, even if it's only a one-time coffee one.

The wisdom lies in knowing who to turn down at the beginning to save you both time and possible rejection and who to respond to, in the hopes that there will be a spark. How do you get this wisdom? I wish it were just from reading these missives. But unfortunately, it is usually from having lived through a few experiences where you have to turn someone down for a second date, knowing you should have done so before the first. knowing you should have done so before the first.

Making the rounds

I feel like a doctor making her hospital rounds checking on patients. But instead of looking in on Mr. Hernandez after his gallbladder surgery, or Mrs. Fukumoto after her hemorrhoid removal, I check on D1ForU, DreamBeau, LoverBoy1951. I go from Match.com to YahooPersonals to Chemistry.com to SoulMate to see if I have any emails or winks. If I'm really curious, I look at those who've looked at my profile. I do this daily and depending on how bored I am, sometimes more than once.

"Why," you ask, "don't you just let the service notify you when you have an email or flirt/wink/ice breaker?"

Depending on how bored I am, I sometimes check more than once

Good question. While some like eHarmony and Chemistry email you immediately upon someone initiating contact, others aren't as good. It seems there's a lag in YahooPersonals of up to a day. And for some reason I've never received an email from Match telling me someone had made contact, even though I've double checked my notification settings.

"What's the big deal?" you continue. "So what if a guy has to wait a day or two to hear back from you? It's not like he's a customer expecting same-day service."

You're right (which you already knew). In fact, the book *The Rules for Online Dating* says to always wait 24 hours before responding. So what's the rush? Perhaps I have my business customer service quick response system embedded in my brain. I know in business often times the first person to respond to an inquiry gets the business. But in dating, if a guy can't wait a day to hear back

My dating site "Friends"

"He looks so familiar," I think, looking at the man in front of me at the coffee counter. "How might I know him?" My internal search engine Googled my mind looking for a reference to him from one of my social circles. Nothing snapped into place. Until...

"Match.com," I silently exclaimed. "This guy winked at me on Match." Now that he's in front of me, I see he is decidedly shorter than me. "Maybe this is why I didn't converse with him online. Or were there other items that were off putting?"

I debated sharing with him my newly discovered connection. But then, what would I say, "You winked at me on Match.com and I told you we weren't a match"? A not-very-pleasant opening. And if I were to start a conversation, what would I hope to get out of it? I wasn't drawn to his profile, so would I think I'd be drawn to him in person? No, I didn't see any purpose in striking up a conversation with someone I hadn't been interested in knowing online just because he is now standing in front of me. I'd let it pass.

Some of the faces that show up as my matches have appeared for the nearly 3 years I've been online dating. I've read their profiles often searching for something that might entice me to contact them, I have memorized some parts. "Ah, yes, the transplanted Brit," I remember as I reread the profile with the cute pic. But then as I scan his other pics I see his primary photo must be 20 years old, but he chose that one to advertise to the dating world. A bit of a deception, I think, and move on.

"This guy has such beautiful daughters," I remind myself as I click on another's profile." "And this one is also from my home state." I can recite some facts by heart about a few.

I attended the same event as one of my dating site "friends," with whom I've never corresponded. But I knew a lot about him. I rehearsed how I'd introduce myself when there was a break in the program. Without disclosing how I knew him I'd say, "You look like a man who loves restoring old cars. I'm getting a feeling you're working on a red '72 Corvette right now. Is that right? And you like to cook, especially Italian. Yes? And I'm guessing you're in real estate." When he looked confused at how I could know so much about him I'd tell him my screen name. But alas, he was gone before I could toy with his mind.

I do wonder what I'd do if I ran into one of these virtual "friends." Would I say anything? Or, like with

the coffee house encoun-
ter above, would I just
keep my mouth shut. So
much depends on the
circumstance. If he were
with others, I'd pass on
by, as I wouldn't want to
embarrass him if being
on a dating site was something he didn't want oth-
ers to know. And, vainly,

*So much boils
down to vanity*

it would also depend on if I looked good that day. Some
days after exercising, with no make up, I'm not feeling
I'd make a great first impression. And after all, I'd want
him thinking, "Darn, why didn't I ever contact her," ver-
sus "Man, I dodged a bullet by not asking her out." So
much boils down to vanity, doesn't it?

Do you begin to think of these guys who perpetu-
ally show up in your matches as people you know? If
you ran into one of them, what would you do?

Let the games begin

As I respond to an interesting potential suitor's email today, I hear myself saying the command heard at the start of the Olympics. I'm don't like to think of dating as a game — although there are gamelike parts. I work hard to not play games in dating, even though there are plenty of those who do.

What I mean by the line is that once you respond positively to someone's initial inquiry (or he to yours), it sets off a series of emails, often fun and flirty. If you pass muster with each other, you progress to a phone call, then if that is acceptable, a meeting. In each interaction, you want to display your personality, while simultaneously working to be on your best behavior (if you're at all conscious).

Responding positively sets the dating "game" in motion. I wish there were a better metaphor, as the word game used in reference to dating is so negative. But you know what I mean — a loosely prescribed set of actions.

But in this game, the rules are not agreed to by all the players, which leads to assumptions, frustration and disappointments. Sometimes the players appear to be playing very different games, but they're doing it on the same field. And one can't understand why the other is doing X because it makes no sense in the rules they are playing by.

Since the rules are nebulous, it is unclear when one is winning. In dating, ideally you both win. But some have agendas like, "If I can get him to buy me a drink, I win," "If I can get her number, I win, "If he takes me to a nice restaurant, I win," "If I can get her to kiss me, I win," "If he buys me jewelry, I win," or "If I can get her in bed, I win."

> *Since the rules are nebulous, it is unclear when one is winning*

And any player can leave the game at any time, and they do, often without informing the other player. One declares, "Game over," but only in his/her head.

So it is hard to allow the games to begin when you don't want to play any manipulative mind games. The best you can do is try to adapt to the situation as you experience it with the other, so you are co-creating the rules of the game for the two of you.

A missing link in online dating: social-circle accountability

We've heard — and sometimes experienced — the horror stories of midlife dating. When we think that middle-aged men and women should behave like adults they flummox us with their adolescent behaviors.

Many of these bad boy/girl stories come from meeting folks through Internet dating sites. If you've been around for more than a day, you realize that not everyone listed on a site has stellar ethics and social skills. They do things that leave us incredulous — whether it's happened directly to us or we hear about it from someone else.

It's made me ponder the various reasons why people act the way they do when in dating mode. Is it lack of social skills education, not caring how they affect another, or general self-centeredness and obtuseness? I have a theory to add to these.

Lack of social-circle accountability.

> *The friend has determined the person to be socially adept*

When you meet someone through friends, some filtering happens beforehand. If you meet your date at a friend's party, the friend has determined the person to be socially adept enough to be in their circle. Granted, someone else could have brought the guy along, but they would have assessed he's not a total creep as they wouldn't want him embarrassing them at the party.

Secondly, there is built in social accountability. If you or he is a jerk to the other, the friends will hear about it. "What's with Fred? We set a lunch date then he never showed." Or "Is there something going on with Alice? I asked if she'd like to go out and she said yes, but she has yet to return my calls."

A pal shared that he asked out a woman he met at some mutual friends' party. They had a wonderful dinner a week later, and a few days after that he invited her to his house for pizza and a DVD. She accepted and they set the time. She didn't arrive. He called her cell 15 minutes after her due time. No answer. He called again at 30 minutes, then an hour after her expected arrival. He was concerned for her safety. He emailed her the next day to ask what happened. No response.

A week later, he asked some mutual friends if she was okay. They said she was and had no idea why she would stand him up. They checked with her, then got back to him. She said he was physically aggressive and she was concerned about going to his house. This is totally out of his character (I know this guy and he's a good one). Why couldn't she just decline his second invitation if that was how she felt? Instead, she started this rumor mill.

Their mutual friends had known him much longer than her, he'd dated other women in their extended social circle, and there had been no reports of his being inappropriate with anyone. (We know that some people can be entirely different in public settings than they are behind closed doors. We also know he could have been inappropriate with other women in the circle and they didn't speak out.) However, other examples of this woman making stuff up was beginning to surface. She was caught lying about other things.

They were both accountable to their social circle. If there had been other evidence of my pal being inappropriate, he would have been ostracized by the group. I realize this doesn't happen in all groups; some let egregious behavior (e.g., adultery, abuse) slide. But many groups will police their own and shun social misfits. And some will confront him/her directly.

In Internet dating, some people behave as they never would in person (if you're communicating by IM, email or phone). And when they meet you, they do and say stuff they wouldn't try if you met them through a friend.

What have you experienced in social circle accountability? Have you seen representatives from a group step in when there has been unacceptable behavior when two of its members are dating?

He wants to get sexual — online!

An Adventures in Delicious Dating After 40 reader writes:

> *This has happened a few times so am wondering if it is just me, or is common with midlife guys — or just midlife guys on online dating sites. We begin a fun banter via email or IM. I don't get dirty with them, just playful. Some time passes — anywhere from an hour to a few weeks. We haven't met. Their IMs go from playful and flirty to dirty, telling me what they want to do to me, or what they imagine us doing naked, etc., often graphically.*

> *I say I don't want to go there. They persist. I sign off. They apologize. Then they start again.*

> *If I don't care about the guy, I block his IMs. But if I liked him before he went porno on me, I think I ought to give him a second chance. Should I just put my foot down and say I'm uncomfortable going there? Or should I play along, knowing I'll never meet some of them anyway? If I play along and then we agree to meet, I'm afraid he'll jump me as soon as we say hello.*

The question is, what do you want? Sounds like you don't want to have a cybersexual relationship, so why tolerate a guy's going there? If you say no and he persists, he isn't honoring your preferences or boundaries and will be continually pressing you even when you say no.

I think you're right about those you'd meet in person. They will already think you are a loose woman and try to get a home run soon after saying hello. I've made the mistake of being too flirty with a guy on email, and then when we met he wanted me to go back to his place. No thanks, buddy!

Remember, some guys are online dating who would never be dating the normal way because they are socially stunted and very few women would go out with them. So the only way they can get any titillation with a live women without paying is through dating sites. So if you are friendly and engaging, they are going to go for it even at the risk of not meeting you in person.

There is nothing in it for you to go there, as that will end nearly all non-sexual conversation. You'll be the equivalent of an unpaid 900-number worker. So I wouldn't even entertain the notion.

Cyber suitors: What do you call him when you haven't met yet?

his online dating business has created a quandary. For example, how do you refer to a man you've never met who lives 400 miles away and has called nearly every day — sometimes twice a day — for 4 months?

How do I refer to him when I talk to friends? I don't usually share potential suitors' names with friends until I've at least met a guy and know he's going to be around for a while. He's not "my guy" or "beau" or even "man I'm seeing" since we haven't yet met.

How do I refer to him when I talk to friends?

In the old days it was somewhat simpler. Unless you were starting a long-distance romance via mail after having been "introduced" by friends or family, you had both met and could call him your "gentleman caller," "suitor," "fella," or most commonly, "guy I'm dating." With virtual introductions being more common, it has left us with a language void. My teenaged nieces would say that "we're talkin'" but there's no word to describe him.

"Cyber suitor" or "virtual boyfriend" don't quite capture it, but perhaps it's a start.

Skanks-R-Us

You've been dating for a while. You've had lots of first dates that didn't evolve to seconds. So your dating numbers seem high to those who've been out of the dating scene for years. To them any number over 10 seems outrageous if you exclude anything before age 30.

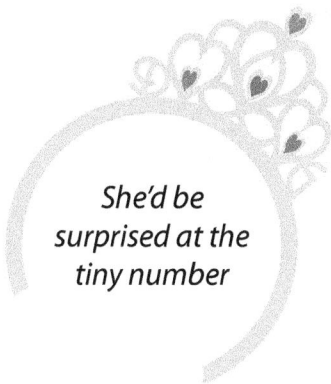

She'd be surprised at the tiny number

They assume you are a skank. Yesterday, at lunch with a group of women I barely knew, a woman asked, "Of those you've dated since your divorce, how many have you slept with?" I didn't tell, as it was none of her business, but she'd be surprised at the tiny number.

But people think that because you have gone out with a lot of people that means you have also slept with a lot of people. "Dating" means "sex" to them, and it appears they think indiscriminate sex, easy sex, or promiscuousness. In other words, you're a skank.

I know some women fall into bed easily. That is their choice. I am taken aback, however, at the assumption by people who don't even know me that I fall into that category. It really says more about them that they would determine my skankiness having no information about me or my discernment.

So how do you deal with nosy or assumptive people speculating about your morals and behavior? Mostly, just ignore them, or if you prefer to be more forthright, say "It's really none of your business." But if you want to be clear, polite and make your point, simply say, "Many fewer than you'd imagine."

When to remove your online profile?

You've been dating your guy for a little while — perhaps 1-3 months. You like him a lot and he seems to like you similarly. You have no interest in seeing anyone else, and he says he isn't seeing anyone else. He asks you what he says to men who email you, and you say, "Thank you but I'm seeing someone right now." He says he does the same thing to the women who contact him.

So why is his profile still visible on the dating site? And for that matter, why is yours?

This subject of when to remove or hide your online profile is a tricky one. If one of you removes your profile and the other doesn't, it can cause tension. In fact, removing it within the first month of dating can make him think you are more serious — or needy — than he is and may scare him. But not taking it down after having the "exclusivity" discussion can cause more problems.

I remember dating a man for a month before checking the site on which we met to see if I had any new emails to which I needed to respond "No thank you." I was surprised to see that he had been on the site the same day! He'd told me he wasn't dating others, so why was he online? I asked him. He stuttered something unconvincing. While I thought everything was going swimmingly, I could see by his actions that he was still fishing in the pond. I began to check the site daily and noticed he was always on within 24 hours.

I could see that he was still fishing in the pond

So when should you hide or remove your profile? Whenever you're disinterested in meeting others. You don't have to announce this to your guy if you don't want. However, at some point, typically somewhere between 1 and 3 months, if you both say you want to be exclusive, you need to remove your profile from public view. It shows the other you are serious about removing yourself from the dating marketplace. To not do so shows you are still wanting to see who else might contact you.

If you check back a week later and find his profile is still visible to the public, ask him about it. Some sites, like Yahoo!Personals allow you to hide your profile from anyone new, but those who you've had past contact can still see it. So don't log in when you check or you'll still be able to see his profile, even if he's hidden it.

You can hide your profile without actually cancel-ing your account. When you both decide to cancel your accounts — to all the sites on which you're listed, not just the one on which you met — it shows a deeper commitment. No, you don't have to be living together or engaged at this point, but be sure that you want to give this relationship all you have. If he balks at cancel-ing, he's not serious.

And if you balk when he asks you to remove your profile or cancel your account, you are still unsure. Let him know. Don't string him along, just as you wouldn't want him to lead you on. The proof is in the profile — or lack thereof.

You never know who'll flirt with you

One of the most fun things about the dating adventure is who you meet serendipitously. It's part of the allure of dating — you never know when a treasure will show up in your in box flirting with you.

This week I've had an encounter that even if it goes nowhere, is still very fun for me.

I am an R&B fan, both oldies and new artists. So last year when I briefly dated an R&B disk jockey (see "Living an R&B song" in the book *Dipping Your Toe in the Dating Pool: Dive In Without Belly Flopping*), I was thrilled because this man immersed himself in my favorite music and emceed events with my most-liked artists. He promised to take me to some of the concerts, but went poof before he could deliver.

Imagine how fun it was this week for me to be contacted by a man who is part of a still performing famous oldie R&B group which has several well-known songs you'd recognize. We've only connected by phone and email and he's been charming. He's sent me several YouTube video links featuring him singing with the group.

Upon viewing the videos of the group in brightly colored suits, I wonder if I own the wardrobe to date a performer. Luckily, none of his outfits are sequined, but I'm not used to dating a man who wears orange, gold and bright blue suits — with matching shoes! I have red, teal, and plum suits, so am wondering if we'd have to coordinate colors before a date so we don't clash!

Thankfully, he assures me that he only wears the vividly hued attire on stage. No need to be concerned at the looks we would attract with a man dressed in red from head to toe.

Watching him dance on stage in the videos, I decided he could teach my Jazzercise instructor a few steps. But what about when we go dancing — will I have to learn the dips, spins, and hand movements that he is used to?

This man is out of my geographical range, so even if it is a brief diversion, it's fun to enter his world, if only just virtually.

(Yes, I know that anyone can post a picture of anyone online and then link to a video, so this person could just be posing as this singer. I have no evidence that he's not who he says he is and have asked him enough questions about his life style that so far it makes sense. But I will be watching for any signs that he's an impostor.)

He asks you for money

nfortunately, this is becoming more common. And not just with men who list themselves from Nigeria or London — hot spots for scams (Nigerian scammers claim to be from London sometimes) — but from others who represent themselves as all-American.

A gal pal's friend was contacted by a man on a dating site who said he was deployed in Iraq. After 6 weeks of daily sweet emails and deepening phone conversations, it happened. He was coming back to the US, he said, and got stuck in Guam. Some mishap happened and he was $2500 short in getting back to the US, where they could finally meet. Could she wire him the money?

Luckily, this midlife woman knew enough to say no. And she cut off all contact with him. I have no idea how he got around the fact that the US military would bring him home so he wouldn't need additional funds, but I don't know all the details.

It's happened to me as well. After 10 days of talking to a man, supposedly a CEO of a 40-person firm in my city, he was called away on business overseas for a week. So our first meeting would be postponed until he returned. But he didn't skip a beat calling, IMing and emailing romantic messages every day. While away, he was assigned an immediate relocation to — you guessed it — Nigeria. He would only be in my town for less than 48 hours to close up his house and get ready for his 6-month relocation. He promised he'd make time for us to meet during this whirlwind visit. He didn't.

During this virtual wooing, he said he'd like us to start a business together, as I had a good business mind. I said we'd discuss it down the road. Once he knew he was going to Africa, he said he'd like us to import African art. I said we could discuss it at a later date. A few days after landing in Africa, he called excitedly telling me what beautiful sculptures he'd discovered. He'd negotiated a 75% discount and had put money down for the first pieces. He investigated that we could sell these in the US for $400,000. He just needed the $12,000 balance. Could I send it to him?

No. I would not be sending $12,000 half way around the world to a man I hadn't met for art I hadn't seen for a business I didn't want to be in. What kind of idiot did he think I was?

Yet women (and men!) fall for these scams all the time. When someone calls you "honey," "sweetie," "sweetheart," and "darling" before they've even met you, that is a yellow flag. When someone tells you he's falling in love with you but hasn't met you, more yellow flags. When he seems to shower you with affection you crave, another yellow flag. But when he asks you for money — any amount of money — that is a red flag. Game over. Move on.

Picture causes interest loss

Adventures in Delicious Dating After 40 reader
Steve asks:

> *What is the best approach when you begin email-
> ing someone from an online dating site, get in-
> terested, then exchange photos and lose most of
> your interest because the person is unattractive to
> you? Is this something worth pursuing? Sometimes
> people look better than their photos. Sometimes as
> we get to know someone better we become more
> attracted to that person. However, if there is no or
> very little attraction based on the photo despite the
> interesting email exchanges, is it worth pursuing
> the relationship?*
>
> *There's something backwards about online dating.
> You get to know the person before you ever find out
> if there's a physical spark.*

Dear Steve:

I've had this exact same issue. If a guy doesn't have
a pic posted but his profile sounds interesting, when he
makes contact I request a photo saying, "Please email
me a pic so I can see with whom I'm communicating.

After all, you have a pic of me." If he doesn't comply, something is amiss so I stop responding.

If he sends a pic and he is totally unappealing, I pull back significantly not asking him any questions hoping the communication dies. If I need to, I say something directly about not feeling we're a match.

That said, I have met with some men who were much more appealing in person than their pictures, as I explained in "Clothes make the man." But that has been the exception rather than the rule.

Some men were much more appealing in person.

If you have the time and interest to meet the person, only commit to coffee, as usual. If you've developed some fondness on email or the phone, it would be easy to suggest dinner or a longer initial meeting. But stick to something short so you can extricate yourself gracefully if there's no appeal in person.

Dating a fur ball

There are so many men with many pictures of their dogs on their profiles it makes me wonder if I will be dating their dogs. One man who interested me wrote so glowingly about his dog, I started my communication to him by writing to his dog. The dog wrote back and we had a very fun correspondence. Unfortunately when we met, the man was not as enticing as his dog!

Another beau's affection for his toy poodles drove me batty. He baby-talked to them incessantly and it was far from masculine and alluring. He was a horrible housekeeper and there was dog hair everywhere. I had to watch what I wore to his house otherwise when I left my clothing would be as furry as the dogs. Same with his car.

I like dogs and cats as they can be fun and loving. But I don't like when a dog jumps on me when I'm dressed up. Nor do I like smelly cat litter boxes, nor clouds of fur.

Most people adore their pets. I think it's key that someone you are considering dating seriously at least tolerates your pet. An ex-beau hated cats. When I was a cat owner, he meanly pushed the cat away when the cat tried to say hello.

If you think of your pets as your furry kids, be up front that your pet is very important to you.

And if you're not the pet owner, at some point you will be spending time with your sweetie's pet, either at his house, or if the pet is a dog, walking at the park, beach or neighborhood. So whether your sugar's pet is a dog or cat, learn to carry a lint roller, as you'll be using it a lot. And bringing the pet treats can help you win its owner's heart, too.

Dating profiles for the writing inept

If you've scanned any online profiles, you've probably been shocked at how poorly written 98% of them are. It seems few people can 1) write a coherent, typo-less sentence, and 2) describe themselves accurately and compellingly.

Enter a new service: ProfileWiz. Their press release describes it as:

"… a new service that produces a 500-word personalized dating profile in less than five minutes. The site poses 22 questions and presents possible answers in the forms of photos. Simply select the photo that answers such queries as "What sparks a conversation with you?" or "If you had an extra hour today, what would you do?"

"When completed, the quiz produces a written profile that illuminates the user's personality, dating preferences and desires. The profile is fully customizable, as ProfileWiz offers interchangeable sentences to describe key attributes which can be selected or modified by the user to reflect their unique tastes, mood, humor and attitude. Like having your own, personal Cyrano de Bergerac to pen your profile, the site is capable of writing more than 64.1 trillion possible combinations to ensure the profile is both unique and engaging."

I tried it. The output actually is pretty good. You can customize any part, writing in your own words or clicking through their suggestions for the heading or specific paragraphs. Here's what the site generated for my first paragraph:

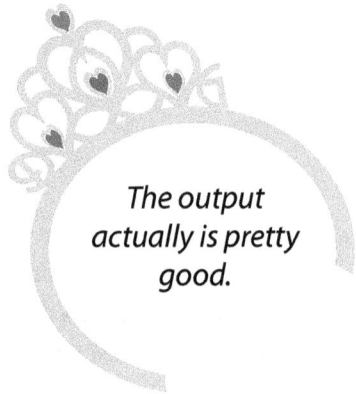

The output actually is pretty good.

"Neat, Intelligent, Clean, Easy-going girl here… (See what I did there?) I'm also a pretty fun to hang out with and, perhaps you can tell, I don't take life too seriously. There's a part of me that's really calm and peaceful. I really like getting close to nature and exploring in the great outdoors! As for my take on life, I'm a natural organiser and thrive on being busy. I get a real kick out of having lots to do." Since I would never call myself a "girl," I could change that. Nor would I use initial capitals after a comma, or put an explanation point after "outdoors," but I am a writer and editor.

And it sounds like I'm a granola gal, hiking up muddy hills every weekend. Nope, not me. My heels get stuck in the mud! So I could take out the emphasis on that, and in fact, can retake the assessment to see what it would generate if I chose fewer outdoor photos.

You can export your profile to easily plunk into any dating site.

A nit to pick, which I've reported to the developers, is a few of their questions don't match what is generated. For example, it asks to select an image of a great date, so I selected bumper cars which I think are fun. But the profile translated that to "my idea of a good first date is something a bit light-hearted and wacky." Actually, my first date ideal is someplace where we can talk and interact, which we couldn't do on bumper cars. That would be good for a second date, not a first date.

And of course it generalizes since the profile is based on your responses to 22 questions. So when I chose a foreign beach locale as my dream life, the profile said, "My dream life? Simple really — sun, sea, sand. Not a care in the world. Care to join me on my desert island?" Well, my dream life is being a citizen of the world, not only living on a beach.

It's written in British English, so if you're in the US, you'll have to take out extra "u"s and other British spellings. Another nit-pick — for some reason some sentences don't have a space after the period. Odd.

But generally, I think the text generated is much, much, much better than what most folks post on sites. So if you feel you're writing impaired, try it, then change the parts that don't reflect you accurately. You profile will stand out among the dreck!

It was bound to happen

In my five-plus years of dating, I've connected with thousands of men from various dating sites. Some have only been through email, others progressed to a phone call, and I've actually met face-to-face with 101 of them.

I've never run into any of the ones who didn't make it to the coffee date.

Until today.

A man attended my seminar who looked vaguely familiar. Then his voice struck a chord. How did I know him? I wracked my brain. Then it struck me clearly — I had talked to him after we went through the eHarmony get-to-know-you process. In fact, he's one of just a handful who talked to me via Skype video chat so his mannerisms were clearer than if we'd just talked by phone.

It was a bit awkward for me throughout the seminar to know that he and I had toyed with the possibility of dating. But I didn't get a sense that he recognized me.

Afterward, I asked him if he lived in the nearby town where I thought he was from. He said he did. Bingo. Then I said I had a question for him I'd ask when everyone had cleared the room. He was intrigued. I asked if he'd ever been on eHarmony and he said yes. I shared that we'd chatted one night. He smiled, but didn't remember the connection. No problem, as I was surprised myself since we'd only had one conversation.

So now that we've officially met, am I interested in getting to know him better? Not really. He seemed like a nice enough guy, and his comments in the session were intelligent and articulate, but I wasn't drawn to him. And he made no sign he would be interested in getting to know me better either.

So we will see. I have a rule about not dating clients, and although he's not technically a client, he is the employee of one. So even if we were both interested in getting to know one another more, it would have to wait until I was done with this 2-month engagement.

Have you ever run into someone you'd met virtually from a dating site but never met in person?

Getting back on the online dating train

After one has been dating for a while, the excitement and novelty of meeting new people wears off. Couple that with too many one-time-only encounters, and you become more guarded with your time and emotions.

At least I know this is true for me, and I'm guessing it is for others who have been searching for their next mate for years.

I've slowed down considerably my dating activities. The last new man I went out with was 8 months ago. And while we became fast friends, I know it will never advance beyond that. He's got some deal breakers that are insurmountable for me and he knows it. So we enjoy a bi-weekly chat, but it's become an unpaid mutual business coaching session.

I'd pulled back on my online dating activities, as I was getting too many men contacting me who were geographically, economically, educationally, or emotionally not a match. So it was with mixed emotions that I decided to rejoin Match.com this week.

Over a year ago I canceled my subscription because the same faces were appearing over again and I had already either ruled them out, had contacted them to no response, or met them and felt no connection. I felt I'd exhausted that pool.

So why did I rejoin? Match.com merged with Yahoo Personals so thought there may be some new possibilities. I searched for local men in my age range and hundreds of new faces emerged. After reactivating my profile, I immediately got a handful of contacts. So I renewed. I then searched by even more specific criteria, and lots of possible matches appeared. I've been merrily emailing and responding to emails.

We'll see if this time my efforts are more fruitful.

I stay in the online dating game because I have met some wonderful men, even if many of them are geographically undesirable. I'm meeting one in a few weeks when I'm in his area since we've been talking weekly for a few months. In a few months, I will finally meet another who's flirted with me for a year. Why bother with these men who will most likely never turn into romantic mates? Because they are interesting, articulate, intelligent, funny and good conversationalists. We've met in an unlikely way yet found enough commonalities to keep us delighting in our banter and discussions.

Will my foray back into Match.com yield my King Charming? Stay tuned!

Online dating behaviors studied

A recent article shared conclusions from researchers at UC Berkeley's School of Information. The paper "Self-presentation and Deception in Online Dating" found pretty much what we've known all along. For example:

Men are more likely to make the first move, sending that first "wink" or email. They're quicker to respond to women's queries.

Women responded to only 16 percent of messages, and they take longer to respond.

Both genders seek partners similar to themselves in age, education, height, religion, politics and views about smoking.

Women are less open-minded, at least regarding ethnicity. They're twice as likely as men to specify that they're seeking someone of their own ethnicity.

Both sexes tell white lies. Men say they are a half-inch taller. Women shave five pounds off their weight.

Women's profiles related more to home, sex and emotions; men's profiles talked about work.

A photograph is the dominant predictor of whether men will connect. Women value narratives in profiles in addition to pictures.

Some of this information was garnered by content analysis of people's actual online behavior. They tracked people's actions (who initiated contact, how long it took to respond, words in profiles). But they must have interviewed daters to get the info on what was attractive in a profile, their true height and how much they really weighed.

In another study reported in the Journal of Personality and Social Psychology, published by a team from Harvard Business School, Boston University and MIT, the conclusion was that less is more in how much is shared in a profile. Their reasoning: when a lot of information is exchanged, more differences are exposed and there is less attraction.

Now this conclusion I found interesting. I am not drawn to men who say nearly nothing in their profiles. I want to know what's important to them. It is true that some of them disclose things that prompt an immediate delete but I think that is good that I don't waste time on people who share something I find repelling. I share a lot in my profile, even though I know most men don't read much of a woman's profile. I want those who do to know as much about me as can be shared in a written essay.

What do you think of these two studies? Anything here but common sense?

My online dating research

I'd read data that said 50% of men listed on dating sites never get one contact from women.

Yet my experience is that men rarely respond to my being the one who makes the initial contact, or for the few who do, it's nearly all "thanks but no thanks."

So I decided to set up an experiment. Granted, it's not very scientific, as I only posted one profile and set of pictures. Had I been more scientific, I would have posted various ones to see if it was my looks or writing that was alluring or repelling.

For the last 3 months, I've regularly emailed men I thought had some chance of being a match. The results are dismal.

I emailed 100 men, all within a 50-mile radius. I met their age, height, education and body-shape criteria.

Out of the 100 men, 47 looked at my profile, sometimes more than once.

Ten sent a "Thanks, but I've just started seeing someone and want to see if it works out" email. Has this become the new standard message for "We're not a match"?

One struck up an email and phone conversation and we met for a drink. We were not a match.

So what's up with this data? If men rarely receive contact from a women, why would 53% of them not even look at my profile? Were they already seeing someone but haven't hidden or removed their profile? Too busy to even look at what someone sent them?

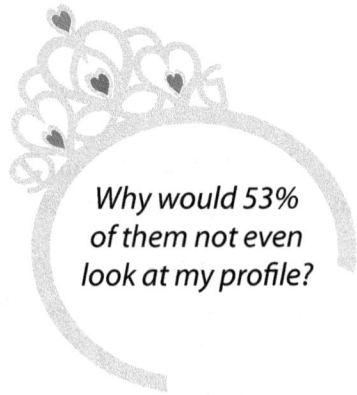

Why would 53% of them not even look at my profile?

Ten percent had the decency to acknowledge my overture. I believe if someone has taken the time to reach out, I owe them at least a response. Obviously, that's not a common feeling.

People ask me if I've been successful with online dating. I always say it depends on your definition of "success." In this example, I had a 99% failure rate — 100% if you count the guy I met that wasn't a match. Is that success? In the past, I've met nearly all my guys through dating sites. Some have become beaus. Most were one-meeting only encounters. Is that success?

My feeling is I would have gone out with many fewer men if I depended on the "natural" way of meeting in a class, at a coffee shop, or through friends. These methods have resulted in nearly no dates. So online dating has allowed me to meet many more men, with some working out at least for a while.

So what's a woman to do who wants to be proactive rather than wait for a man who interests her to make contact? I will still email interesting men, just not as diligently now knowing the odds. It is frustrating to realize that men still like to initiate, yet my experience reflects that with nearly all of my beaus being the first contacters.

A date with a shepherd

I am a bit of a job snob, tending to eschew men who I don't feel have a similar job status. I'm not proud of it, but it's true. I've tried dating blue collar men, and I've never found it worked well.

So you'll be surprised to learn that I had a first date with someone on the other end of the career spectrum — a shepherd.

Where does one even find such a rarity? Online. No, there is not a ShepherdDatingCentral.com — although there is a site for dairy farmers in England.

He was a high-level manager in a high-profile company for 30 years before retirement. Which is when he took up shepherding. He's educated, intelligent, articulate, cultured — he just happens to enjoy doing sheep herding and shearing demonstrations since it's a bit of a dying art in the US.

He and I had been in contact for many months, emailing and talking on the phone, since we enjoyed each other's conversation.

But as you can guess, he doesn't live in a large city, as there is little call for shepherds there. So he lives in a remote part of the country, near which I was working recently. I told him of my upcoming visit and he said he'd drive the 2.5 hours to come meet me. I then shared that my dilemma was how to get from my client's city to another remote town several hours from his, as a friend had invited me to visit her there. He offered to come fetch me (herd me?) and drive me — in a car, not running while being nipped at by his dogs — to her town, even though it would be a 5 hour drive from where I was working, and another 2 hours home for him.

He said he'd drive the 2.5 hours to come meet me.

He — and his two Border collies — arrived at the appointed time and we embarked on our adventure. He regaled me with stories of the gentleman shepherd's life (he lives in a comfortable house on acreage where his sheep graze and he and the collies sleep inside, of course). I learned all I could hold about lambing, shearing, herding, tagging and selling sheep. Luckily, he had a broad range of conversation topics so we ebbed and flowed easily. The five hours passed quickly.

When I shared with a friend of his offering to drive me the five hours, she seemed incredulous that someone would do this for a stranger. I responded, "I have some allure." Afterward she asked how it was. I told her it was fun and that he said it was the highlight of his month, she responded, "Must be a slow month." Aren't friends grand?

Will I see the shepherd again? We live too far apart to try to strike up a romance. If we are in each other's neighborhood, we could have dinner. But he is much more of a mountain man than I am a mountain woman. While I enjoy the outdoors, I don't relish camping and long hikes, nor am I fond of cold. So we will remain pals.

Have you dated someone in a profession that you thought you'd never consider? How did it work out?

Resources

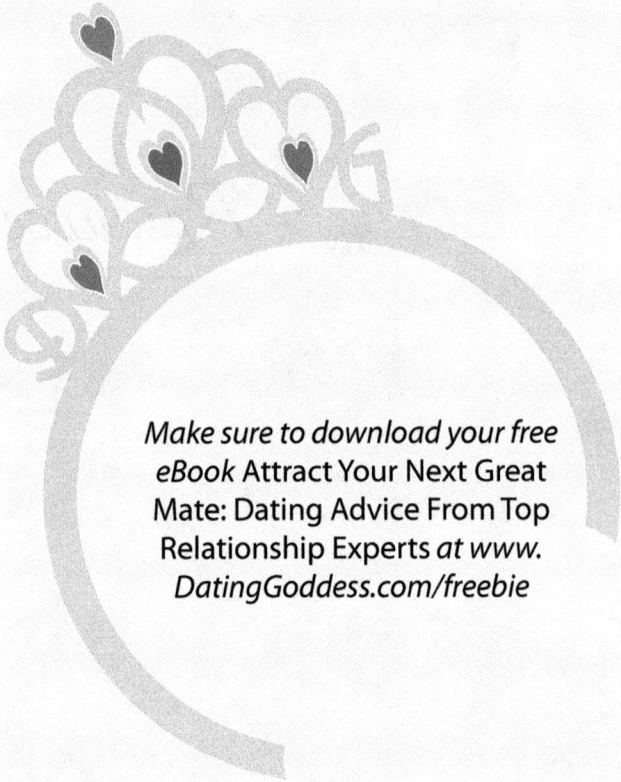

Make sure to download your free eBook Attract Your Next Great Mate: Dating Advice From Top Relationship Experts *at www. DatingGoddess.com/freebie*

Afterword

At the time of this writing, I have not yet found my true King Charming. I continue my search with verve. I've become more discerning about what I want and don't want. I've met some wonderful men pals — my treasures — who continue to be in touch.

I wish you much luck in your adventure. It will be fun and frustrating, exhilarating and exasperating, and sexy or sexless. So much depends on you, your approach and your attitude. My books are designed to help you enjoy as much as possible and ward off unpleasantness. But nearly all adventures have wonderful highs as well as a few lows. If you know that going in and arm yourself with information on what to expect, you'll have more of the positives and fewer of the negatives.

Please drop by www.DatingGoddess.com and join in the discussion and report on your experiences.

Dating Goddess

R*esources*

Go to www.datinggoddess.com to access a variety of useful resources. We work to suggest resources we think have value.

Dating and relationship book reviews

These reviews will save you time and money as I've given you my take on specific books, CDs and more. Some are worth your effort to buy and read or listen to them — some are not. We're always adding new book reviews, so check frequently. We'll also notify our mailing list when new resources are added.

Dating site links

There are a lot of dating sites on the Internet. I've listed the ones I think are worth investigating.

Dating products and tools

Dating can be daunting. We're continually looking at

ways to make it easier and more fun. We'll provide info on games, tools, even date-wear that will help others know you're available, or help you get to know potential suitors better.

Dating and relationship advice sites

Advice "experts" abound on the Internet as anyone can self-proclaim themseves as expert — even if they haven't dated in 30 years and never in midlife. I've worked to find experts who's advice I generally think is solid.

Midlife recources

We'll feature Web sites, books, events and other resources we think might interest you.

Newly discovered resources

I'll add other resources as we discover them, subscribe to our mailing list to get the scoop as soon as we find them. Go to www.DatingGoddess.com to register for our mailing list. Don't worry, we won't sell or give your email to anyone.

Acknowledgments

 et me start by acknowledging the 112 men who helped trigger the lessons contained in this book. Some prompted several! They remain nameless here to protect their identity, although most would recognize references to them. Plus the thousands more whose winks, emails and calls didn't result in a date, but helped me learn the dating game. And all those men who I emailed who never responded — such a blessing to have them weed themselves out.

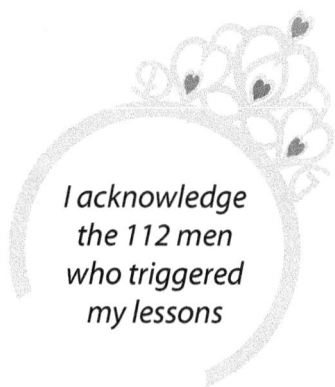

I acknowledge the 112 men who triggered my lessons

I'd like to thank my Seven Sisters mastermind group for the tremendous brainstorming, noodling, strategizing and encouragement. I wouldn't have begun this project without the prodding of Val Cade, Chris Clarke-Epstein, Mariah Burton Nelson, Sue Dyer, Sam Horn and Marilynn Mobley.

Thank you to my good friends who've listened to my dating stories ad nauseam, and whose support and wisdom are embedded in this text. Ed Betts, Ken Braly, Bruce Daley, Tom Drews, Elaine Floyd, Paulette Ensign, Scott Friedman, Craig Harrison, Mary Jansen, Tom Johnson, Sandy Jones, Mary Kilkenny, Ellie Klevins, Patrick Lynch, Mary Marcdante, Barbara McNichol, Ann Peterson, Anthony Ramsey, Caterina Rando, Kristy Rogers, Jana Stanfield, Holly Steil, Terry Tepliz, and George Walther, thank you.

The Adventures in Delicious Dating After 40 series

The *Adventures in Delicious Dating After 40* series is designed to help you understand your own midlife dating journey. It is not a road map, as we all take different routes. It is a guide to help you understand yourself, midlife men, and the dating process. Hopefully, you'll not only learn from the lessons and insights shared in this series, but you'll examine how they apply — or don't — to your own dating adventure.

You'll get the scoop on what you need to know, what's changed since you last dated, and how to navigate inevitable bumps in the road.

Following is an overview of each book in the series and a sampling of some of the chapter titles. All are detailed at www.DatingGoddess.com.

Date or Wait: Are You Ready for Mr. Great?

Are you ready for a special man in your life? You have a great life. But you know you'd like a special man to share it. You think you're ready to date, but you haven't done it in a while.

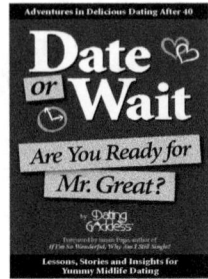

What should you consider before you actually start dating full bore? Even if you've reentered the dating world, this will give you a foundation of attitude and philosophy to make your adventure more fulfilling.

Sample chapters

From hurt to flirt

Dating is like Baskin-Robbins

You've got to kiss a lot of…princes!

What's your definition of dating success?

Are you open to receiving?

Dating: A self-designed personal-growth workshop

Hands-on dating research

Being present to the presents

Being aggressively single

Approaching dating like a buffet

Is Brad Pitt ruining your love life?

Treasures can come in dented packages

Assessing Your Assets: Why You're A Great Catch

You have many wonderful qualities. But it's easy to focus on one's flaws — at least what seem like flaws to you. However, to the right man your imperfections are endearing, attractive and lovable. You have to be clear what you offer a man who will find you enchanting.

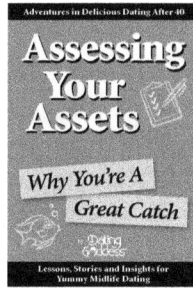

Assessing Your Assets helps you look at what you bring to a new relationship. It will help you see your good points so you'll approach dating with more confidence.

Sample chapters

♥ Don't think you are damaged goods

♥ You are (probably) more attractive than you think!

♥ They aren't called "hate handles"

♥ Are you a good man picker?

♥ What are your deal breakers?

♥ Are you arguing your limitations?

♥ Turn your liabilities into assets

♥ The strong vs. nice woman debate

♥ Is your sense of humor stunting your dating?

♥ Why are we drawn to bad boys?

♥ The zest test

In Search of King Charming: Who Do I Want to Share My Throne?

You are no longer looking for "Prince" Charming because you are a queen. You want someone who is at your level, not groveling at your feet. You want a king — someone who's your equal and with whom you can rule the throne together!

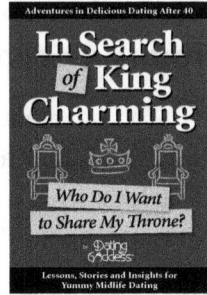

This book focuses on helping you better define what you want beyond tall, dark and handsome! You'll consider characteristics you might not have thought of before. You'll look at what you want now.

Sample chapters

💜 Building your Franken-boyfriend

💜 What's your "perfect boyfriend's" job description?

💜 A man to go with your wardrobe

💜 In search of the elusive good kisser

💜 When you're clear on what you want, it appears

💜 Are you dating the same guy in different bodies?

💜 Does he fit in your world?

💜 What's your kissing quotient?

💜 Is your guy's loving muscle strong?

💜 Do you both have the same dating rhythm?

Embracing Midlife Men:
Insights Into Curious Behaviors

Do you sometimes scratch your head after interacting with a midlife man, wondering, "What could he possibly be thinking?" Especially if it's before, during or after a date with a man who presumably wants to impress you!

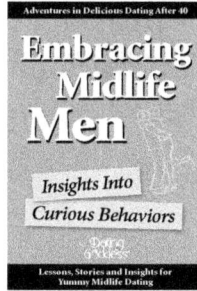

Adventures in Delicious Dating After 40

Embracing Midlife Men

Insights Into Curious Behaviors

Dating Goddess

Lessons, Stories and Insights for Yummy Midlife Dating

This book focuses on better understanding midlife men's behaviors. When you grasp what's going on in his head it's much easier to embrace him. Men are wondrous creatures, so we need to understand them better and love them for who they are.

Sample chapters

💜 Men are like shoes

💜 Why men disappear when it gets serious

💜 Chivalry isn't dead —but it seems to be hibernating

💜 Do men want feisty women?

💜 Midlife men have forgotten how to date

💜 Are you getting prime time from your man?

💜 When a man tells you what he paid for things

💜 Does he treat you like his ex?

💜 Has Greg Behrendt done women a disservice?

💜 Tales of woo

Dipping Your Toe in the Dating Pool: Dive In Without Belly Flopping

You've decided you are ready — you want to start dating. Maybe you've already had a few coffee dates with several men. You want to be as successful as possible on your dating adventure.

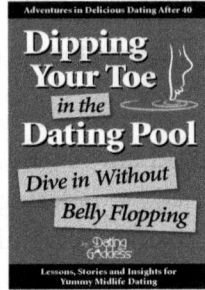

This book focuses on getting started on your dating adventures. We cover what you need to know as you begin your journey.

Sample chapters

💜 Do you have the right datewear?

💜 Dating with integrity

💜 Building your rejection muscle

💜 When "be yourself" is questionable advice

💜 Faux beaus and practice dating

💜 Are you making bad decisions out of loneliness?

💜 Being "in wonder" about your date's behavior

💜 When do you feel most vulnerable in dating?

💜 Are you out of his league — or he yours?

💜 Why listening is so seductive

Winning at the Online Dating Game: Stack the Deck in Your Favor

Internet dating can be frustrating or fruitful. It will be much less exasperating if you know how to read and weed out men's profiles that aren't appropriate for you. And you'll have a steady stream of potential suitors if you know how to write a compelling profile for yourself.

This book focuses on the ins and outs of online dating. How to play the game, which has it's own rules and language. If you don't understand how online dating works, you'll waste a lot of time connecting with men who are not a possible fit for you.

Sample chapters

- Shopping for men
- Safe online dating
- Is 21st Century dating unnatural?
- What do men look at in your profile?
- Euphemisms uncovered
- Are you describing yourself compellingly?
- No, I will not be dating your Harley
- Playing the online dating game
- Scantily clothed pictures

159

Check Him Out Before Going Out: Avoiding Dud Dates

Under the cloak of the anonymity that email and the phone provides, men often reveal more than they intend. If you ask the right questions you can find out a lot about his values and view of the world after just an interaction or two.

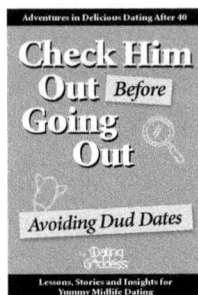

This book focuses on what you need to ask before agreeing to even a coffee date. You need to vet the men who email and call you to ensure you're not likely to waste your time with men who clearly aren't a match.

Sample chapters

💜 Becoming smitten with the fantasy

💜 Can Google help — or hinder — your dating life?

💜 Qualify your potential dates before meeting

💜 The art of consideration

💜 Anticipating a big date is like awaiting Santa

💜 Being seduced by what he is over who he is

💜 Are you his spare?

💜 My boyfriend, whom I haven't met

💜 When canceling is the right thing to do

💜 Politics, religion and sex — oh my!

First-Rate First Dates: Increasing the Chances of a Second Date

You can tell a lot about someone within the first 30 minutes. What does he talk about? Does he ask you questions? If so, what does he want to know about you? What do you need to know about him? How does he treat you? How does he treat those around you?

This book focuses on what goes on during the first date. How do you determine if you want a second date? What you can do to increase the likelihood your date will ask you for a second? That is if you want a repeat!

Sample chapters

💜 Start with coffee

💜 How do you greet him?

💜 When it clicks, throw out some of your criteria

💜 Tracking your date's score

💜 Clues a guy is just looking for a booty call

💜 12 signs he won't be asking for a second date

💜 First-date red flags that this guy isn't for you

💜 Honesty is not always the best policy

💜 Chemistry, or does he make my toes curl?

💜 Women's first-date blunders

Real Deal or Faux Beau: Should You Keep Seeing Him?

You've begun to go out with a man you like. How do you decide if you should continue seeing him, or if you should release him because he's not The One?

This book focuses on second dates and beyond. During the dating process you are both assessing if you want to keep seeing each other. This book helps you determine what questions you need to ask yourself.

Sample chapters

💜 Deciding to see him again or not

💜 What's your date's Delight/Disappointment Scale score?

💜 Broaching tough conversations

💜 "I want to respect me in the morning"

💜 Does he invite you to his place?

💜 Are you stingy in dating?

💜 When his hand is on your knee too soon

💜 Easy way to ask hard questions

💜 Rose-colored glasses obscure red flags

💜 If his stories don't add up, subtract yourself

Multidating Responsibly: Play the Field Without Being A Player

Playing the field is frowned on in some circles. There are definitely appropriate and inappropriate ways to date several men simultaneously.

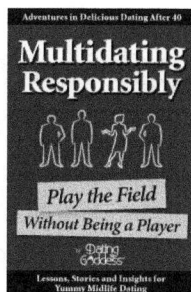

This book focuses on how to date around responsibly and with integrity without leading men on. If you do it with honesty, you can date several people at once until you're both ready to focus only on each other.

Sample chapters

💜 "Pimpin'" — Dating multiple guys

💜 Multi-dating pros and cons

💜 Your Date-A-Base — tracking multiple suitors

💜 "Hot bunking" your beaus

💜 Are you a "Let's Make a Deal" type of dater?

💜 Assume there are other women

💜 Dating's revolving door

💜 How long do you hedge your bet?

💜 Beware of multi-tasking when multi-dating

💜 Back burner beaus

💜 The boyfriend phone

Moving On Gracefully: Break Up Without Heartache

"Breaking up" sounds so high school, doesn't it? But part of the dating process is saying something when one of you decides not to date the other anymore. Going "poof" is not a mature or respectful option in midlife.

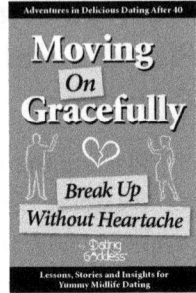

This book focuses on surviving a breakup, whether you initiate it or not. Either way, it's never easy to break up if you have developed any fondness toward the other.

Sample chapters

💜 Hello — goodbye: How to say no thanks after meeting

💜 Releasing back into the dating pool

💜 50 ways to leave your lover? 4 ways not to leave your suitor

💜 Breaking up is hard to do — right

💜 Why men go "poof"

💜 How to trump being dumped

💜 When breaking up is a "Get Out of Jail Free" card

💜 How to detect the end is near

💜 Failed relationships' blessings

💜 He's broken up with you — he just didn't tell you

💜 Rejection is protection

From Fear to Frolic: Get Naked Without Getting Embarrassed

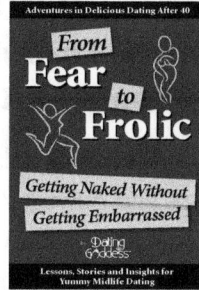

This book focuses on what you need to consider and know before getting physically intimate with a man you're dating. This is nerve-wracking to many midlife women. This book will prepare you.

Sample chapters

💜 Sleepover do's and don'ts

💜 Does he want in your life — or just in your bedroom?

💜 Getting naked with him the first time

💜 An excuse to seduce or how important is bedroom bliss?

💜 What to ask yourself before getting naked with him

💜 Are you and your guy on the same sexual time line?

💜 Sharing your sexual owner's manual with him

💜 What women need from a man before having sex

💜 Why too-soon midlife sex is like non-fat food

💜 How dating sex is like waffles

💜 Too-soon seduction: "I'm special, but not THAT special"

Ironing Out Dating Wrinkles: Work Through Challenges Without Getting Steamed

Nearly all relationships have some ups and downs. Part of getting to know someone is knowing how they work through relationship misunderstandings.

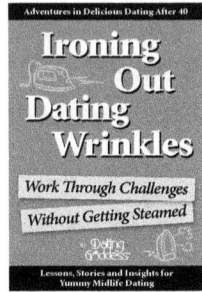

This book focuses on how to work through the inevitable hiccups that happen when you are getting to know each other. If you can both deal with challenges, the bond deepens and you find yourself smitten.

Sample chapters

💜 When your guy vexes you, ask what your highest self would do

💚 The first fight

💜 You want boo; he wants boo-ty

💚 Where's the line between getting your needs met and being selfish?

💜 Expressing your upset with your guy

💜 Is his toothbrush in your cabinet too soon?

💜 Do you love how he loves you?

💜 Is he collecting data on how to make you happy?

💜 Be careful of being smitten

💜 Exclusivity: How and when to broach it

www.ingramcontent.com/pod-product-compliance
Lightning Source LLC
Chambersburg PA
CBHW051730020426
42333CB00014B/1239